I0468476

Eliminate Stress in Your Organization

Strategically Address and Overcome the
External and Internal Stress Factors
that Stagnate Your Organization
and Limit Full Participation
and Success

Jim Koehneke, MA

"We must have a pie.
Stress cannot exist in the presence of a pie."
—

David Mamet, Author

CONTENTS

CHAPTER ONE
Setting the Stage

Introduction

It's a pretty simple formula: if employees are happy, cared about, and supported, productivity is never an issue. And if they are paid really well (instead of having to take two or three jobs to get by) and given paid time off (like many Europeans who get six weeks of vacation and have the money to actually go on vacation), stress is not an issue in the workplace. Well, with one exception: in one country, if a worker is deemed to have stress, they are given a month of paid time off to go live in a spa so they can come back re-invigorated and stress-free.

Or at home, where kids get free education through college, where education focuses on children being children, having fun, and enjoying the feeling of community as the intention of educators instead of on standardized tests that aren't given. Where mothers giving birth are given six months of paid leave to be home caring for their child in the formative years after birth. Where people aren't thrown in jail for using drugs, and when "criminals" do go to jail they are rehabilitated into a community of caring and support (where guards are friendly and where the inmates have their own little "dorm room" of considerable comfort).

And it all begins with how organizations see their relationship to employees, like a partnership that requires dignity and respect rather than as a "tool" to make the organization profit. But, alas, that's not how it is in the US, where the majority of our taxes do not go to pay for free education or free healthcare, but to support the military war machine. So we have to look for other ways to try and reduce stress. And that is the purpose of this book: to suggest ways, given our culture, to cope and even thrive in the face of challenging odds against us. Or at least in comparison to other countries.

The Path to Stress-Free Success

Stress is everywhere. In our personal lives, our homes, and in the workplace. But it needn't be that way. **Whenever a system can eliminate stress, success is the natural result due to greater participation and personal talent being unleashed.** The purpose of this book is to suggest ways to reduce stress and move the culture of an organization to one of aliveness, joyful cooperation, and well-being for the purpose of working toward and expressing a powerful mission. There is no greater condition that your organization could attain than that of well-being. For well-being is the absence of stress that causes individuals and teams to pull back, engage less, and constrict creativity and aliveness.

In order to achieve well-being within our system — as it presently exists today — and create the outcomes we want, a two-pronged approach is necessary. First, organizational/structural factors that cause employee stress need to be addressed and, where appropriate, dealt with. Additionally, there's an ongoing need to teach and coach individuals (at all levels) how to both reduce stress and keep it from entering the picture. I call the latter "preempting stress" — which is done by teaching individuals about the cause of stress and how to heal it. For without stress, well-being flows easily into awareness and opens the gateway for the natural expression of creativity, innovation, and the positive energy of participation leading to success.

This book will address both the structural and personal awareness factors that allow stress to be the continuous and predominant organizational culture by providing top down and bottom up strategies to help employees rise up and experience greater freedom and creative expression found in a stress-free organization.

The Need for Health and Wellness

Health and wellness are now major concerns in our stress-induced society. And stress ("dis-ease") plays a major role in causing many diseases and ailments. Not only is the cost of healthcare substantial for both individuals and organizations, but the effect of poor health has a major effect on worker productivity. While healthy employees show up at work more often than sick ones, happy and inspired employees are significantly more energized, innovative, and productive. It's time we make greater inroads in reducing stress, rather than accepting that "stress is just a normal part of life."

While the literature is abundant and stress management programs can be effective to deal with the *effect* of stress, the problem we must also address is how to eliminate the *cause* of stress. "*Is that even possible, given the nature of society and the world*," you might wonder? While I believe the answer is *'yes'*, changes need to occur on two levels. To reiterate: external causes of stress need to be openly and effectively dealt with to reduce employee anxiety and fear in the workplace. And, secondly, teachings regarding ways to preempt the cause of stress from an internal or mental point of view need to occur, followed by effective individual health coaching to embed new behaviors.

The approach I will cover is intended to support an organization's shift from both inner and outer conflict to one of enthusiasm and high productivity. I will do this by introducing information that gets at reducing the causes of stress in the workplace, as well as our individual lives, so we need not deal with it only after the fact. My goal is to teach people how to live stress-free; that is, avoid stress before it begins. So to that end I will provide a number of strategies to use to preempt stress before it takes hold.

The Effects of Stress on the Body

The below information was adapted from a report of The American Psychological Association.
(http://www.apa.org/helpcenter/stress-body.aspx)

Our bodies are especially vulnerable to stress. The physical reaction to fear and stress can cause all sorts of short-term problems and significant long-term effects. Here's what happens when stress, or *the body's way of responding to any kind of external demand or threat as perceived by the mind*, occurs:

When the body is stressed, the sympathetic nervous system generates what is known as the "fight or flight" response. The body shifts all of its energy resources toward fighting off a life threat, or fleeing from an enemy. The SNS signals the adrenal glands to release hormones called adrenalin and cortisol. These hormones cause the heart to beat faster, respiration rate to increase, blood vessels in the arms and legs to dilate, the digestive process to change, and glucose levels (sugar energy) in the bloodstream to increase to deal with the emergency.

Chronic stress, experiencing stressors over a prolonged period of time, can result in a long-term drain on the body. As the SNS continues to trigger physical reactions, it causes a wear-and-tear on the body. It's not so much what chronic stress does to the nervous system, but what continuous activation of the nervous system does to other bodily systems that become problematic. Below are some examples of how the body deals with stress.

When the body is stressed, the hypothalamus signals the autonomic nervous system and the pituitary gland and the process is started to produce epinephrine and cortisol, sometimes called the "stress hormones." This starts the process that gives your body the energy to run from danger. When cortisol and epinephrine are released, the liver produces more glucose, a blood sugar that would give you the energy for "fight or flight" in an emergency. For some people — especially people vulnerable to Type 2 diabetes — that extra blood sugar can mean diabetes.

When you're stressed, you may eat much more or much less than you usually do. If you eat more or different foods, or increase your use of alcohol or tobacco, you can experience heartburn or acid reflux. Stress or exhaustion can also increase the severity of heartburn pain. When you're stressed, your brain becomes more alert to sensations in your stomach. Your stomach can react with "butterflies" or even nausea or pain. You may vomit if the stress is severe

*enough. And, if the stress becomes chronic, you may develop
ulcers or severe stomach pain even without ulcers.*

*Stress can make you breathe harder. That's not a problem
for most people, but for those with asthma or a lung disease
such as emphysema, getting the oxygen you need to breathe
easier can be difficult. And some studies show that an acute
stress — such as the death of a loved one — can actually
trigger asthma attacks, in which the airway between the
nose and the lungs constricts.*

*Chronic stress, or a constant stress experienced over a
prolonged period of time, can contribute to long-term
problems for heart and blood vessels. The consistent and
ongoing increase in heart rate, and the elevated levels of
stress hormones and of blood pressure, can take a toll on the
body. This long-term, ongoing stress can increase the risk for
hypertension, heart attack, or stroke. Repeated acute stress
and persistent chronic stress may also contribute to
inflammation in the circulatory system, particularly in the
coronary arteries, and this is one pathway that is thought to
tie stress to heart attack. It also appears that how a person
responds to stress can affect cholesterol levels.*

The Result of Untreated Stress

In addition to directly causing health problems, stress is an
indirect cause of numerous other problems. Here are just a few:

- Anxiety and stress lead many individuals to numbing out
the feelings using various substances, causing addictions
ranging from smoking, drugs, and overeating, leading to
obesity.
- Stress on the job leads to more heart attacks on Monday
than any other day of the week.
- Stress for the wage earners in the family leads to poor
performance and reduced financial achievement due to
feeling anxious rather than empowered to succeed.

Any attempt to block stress by numbing the feelings only causes
unwanted stress to return. Continued repression of stress can

also lead to depression. The best thing to do is to admit the truth of what's going on, face it, and take steps to avoid or at least manage the stress as it arises.

This, however, presupposes that the causes of feeling stressed, or even just naming it, can reside out of one's awareness. So expanding awareness is necessary to ensure that the individual not only knows what is happening but also has greater choice in deciding what steps to take to combat or solve the problem. The practice of meditation, among other benefits, can do just that.

While various relaxation techniques, including meditation and the use of audio-technology sound waves, have been shown to increase a sense of well-being and effectively reduce muscle tension, the need to change one's mindset and way of perceiving the world must accompany the behavioral changes if we want to create stress-free workplaces.

An interesting study recently found that the underlying cause of addiction is not necessarily physical dependency on a substance, but rather the absence of a positive environment, including love and support and real connection among caring people. This sheds new light on how to deal with stress; that is, not worry so much about the outer effects but address the human interaction and support environment for people who are stressed or who experience PTSD (Post-Traumatic Stress Syndrome).

Other Benefits of Living in a Stress-Free World

The obvious benefits of eliminating stress in organizations are clear. In addition to having healthier employees that reduce healthcare costs, we get more productive and motivated employees. Another benefit comes as a result of employees in the "right" job — one in which they are both skilled at doing and love to do — that enables creativity and innovation to flourish. As a Career and Life Coach for twenty-five years, my passion has been to help people move toward full self-expression, toward connecting to their authenticity, and creating their lives with passion so they may feel true joy. Stress keeps us focused on trouble ahead, not creative expression in the moment.

While you or I may never get to eradicate stress completely, we can move toward it for the purpose of more powerfully engaging in life and enjoying the fruits of greater self-expression. With less stress in our lives, the more we live! Live to create, contribute, work together, make a difference, and experience success until we go on to a new project or challenge to overcome. Stress stops us and gives us a reason to complain, which equates to *not* living. Far better to experience true aliveness than to sit back and worry about life or what others may think about us. Here is a way to think about what it means to **LIVE**:

> **L**etting one's authentic light shine with creative enthusiasm while overcoming challenges
>
> **I**nvolving oneself in a creative project or goal in which to fully and joyfully engage
>
> **V**oicing an opinion without making others wrong, enabling cooperation and synergy
>
> **E**ngaging what it means to be human: learning, growing, expanding, and serving the needs of others

And if we want to reap the rewards of real joy on earth we each need to take responsibility for reducing and even eradicating stress, both in the workplace and in our own lives.

CHAPTER TWO
External Stressors in Organizations

Overview

Does stress come from outside us? Or is it due to experiences we find ourselves in? Or is stress really about managing thoughts and feeling on the inner level? The simple answer is "both," but in reality acquiring a stress-free mind is ultimately the best answer.

I point this out because certain external stressors in organization can be reduced or eliminated by implementing strategies to reduce the reaction to outside influences, but those strategies will not necessarily permanently change if the same influences return.

The truth is that external stressors in organizations cause low productivity and low morale, but it doesn't have to stay that way. For example, one of the biggest stressors for employees is lack of role clarity, which can change if managers provide clear and direct written information about job responsibilities *and* support the employee in achieving his or her objectives.

Additionally, employees who are in a job that doesn't match their interests, skills, and passions are not only feeling stress but are much less likely to be productive and effective in work than those employees who love what they do. Managers don't necessarily need to weed out the poor performers, but rather help the poor performer find a better match in the organization. Doing this will not only save a great deal of time and cost of replacing them, but will decrease worker stress throughout the organization as employees recognize *"managers care about us and I don't have to be so worried about losing my job."*

Another stressor is the nature or style of management communications to the employees. Managers who act as "coaches" can greatly enhance productivity by listening to employee problems and suggestions and involving employees in decision-making. Taking an autocratic top-down approach typically leads to stress-induced disempowering consequences. This is because employees gain greater motivation by feeling included in the work process and knowing their input makes a difference.

Structural Solutions to Creating Stress-Free Organizations

1. Eliminating External Organizational Stressors

There are many ways to address the external stressors that organizations may not even know they are causing. The key to making change is to recognize and address these stressors so that real productivity and motivation can occur. What's needed first is an effective assessment of what happening "under the surface," creating the opportunity for stress to take hold. And just as important, the willingness of management to understand and accept the data and be willing to make changes where needed.

The most powerful organizational interventions for reducing work stress fall under these four categories:

1. *Leadership Effectiveness Workshops*
2. *Managerial and Executive Coaching*
3. *Increasing Team Motivation and Success*
4. *Getting People in the Right Job*

Leadership Style Makes a Big Difference

The real job of leaders is not to tell or demand employees to do or behave in a particular way, but rather to inspire employees to achieve an important and valued vision. While the "perfect leader" may elude us all, certainly adding in new behaviors can greatly affect employee motivation and productivity. When it comes to managerial approaches and behaviors, below are those that create true **LEADERSHIP** Effectiveness. These approaches can be presented in **Leadership Effectiveness Workshops** and followed up with individual coaching as needed.

> Let your mission be your guide. Develop a vision of the future that focuses on positive outcomes and adds value to the world. Be clear about your strategy, and develop a plan that will turn ideas into reality.

Earn the respect of your team through personal integrity. Stay honest, keep your word, be on time, and do the right thing.

Attend to work with an inspired attitude. Communicate your enthusiasm and speak your commitment to goals in a way that inspires team success.

Determine what resources will best enable your team to achieve your goals. Train and develop people — they are your greatest resource. Be a good coach, support to your team, and ask what you can do to make their jobs easier.

Encourage employees to take creative risks and uncommon action, when appropriate. Help them stretch to greater achievement and enlarge their capacity for achievement.

Retain talent by helping employees grow and develop. Provide career coaching, and help them move to where they can best contribute their purpose, power, and authenticity.

Share problems with your team. Get people involved and participating, and ask them to offer their good ideas and wisdom. Seek out innovative ways to overcome challenges and reach success. Collaborate whenever possible.

Hear issues with an empathetic ear. Care about your employees. Be open, be human, and let people know how you feel.

Investigate progress along the way. Learn from mistakes, and redirect. Do this in small chunks rather than making drastic changes all at once.

Practice celebrating success and rewarding effort. Be specific with praise, and do it often. Don't wait for next quarter's results; do it today.

2. Executive Coaching

If your managers need some help in this area, coaching is very cost-effective. And it works. The results of coaching are renewed energy and enthusiasm, new skills learned and implemented, and improved interpersonal communication. Unlike other management programs aimed at merely teaching theory, coaching creates accountability for change. Key individuals are asked to meet with a Business Coach over a period of time to address some area in which performance improvement, behavioral change, or learning is needed. The coach then works with the key executive until change occurs. Here's why it is so effective:

> **Objectivity.** A good coach is an objective third-party listener, teacher, and partner in the change process. Issues can be dealt with head on, without biased interpretation or recrimination. And the coach becomes a confidante; feelings can be vented and released, opening the way for honesty, openness, responsibility taking, and problem ownership.

> **Learning experience.** Coaching, foremost, is a learning process, in which change can only occur if problem areas are clearly understood. Data is gathered and analyzed, free from the reactive environment of real-life interactions in the workplace. Personality assessment instruments are effectively used to identify "blind spots" that may be contributing to problem areas. And "upward" evaluations, such as 360-degree feedback instruments, can gather information from subordinates and peers, as well as more senior executives.

> **Commitment.** Solutions are jointly sought, and an action plan for change is developed by the executive with the assistance of his or her coach. This plan is then agreed to by upper management so that everyone is in the same game.

> **Practice.** Practice and feedback are crucial to learning and implementing new behaviors, or modifying old habits. While some changes are the result of repetition and the forming of new habits, changed behaviors are *permanently* seated in new

awareness gained over time. As cause and effect relationships are understood, it becomes easier for the exec to step outside negative patterns and implement new behaviors. The coach's job is to act as a guide through this process of practice-feedback-awareness, practice-feedback-awareness.

> **Cost Effective.** Key executives hold a wealth of information and experience necessary to the success of the organization. The loss of valuable knowledge and skills is difficult and costly to replace. Six months of coaching can turn around a problem situation that might otherwise fester until a disgruntled manager either leaves or is asked to leave the organization.

> **Motivation.** Real motivation develops as new possibilities are perceived, new insights are gained, new behaviors are implemented, and new results come about. More than likely the key exec or middle manager is unhappy with the current milieu, and coaching is a chance to step outside or rise above a circumstance that is not working. Individuals being coached respond enthusiastically to the challenge of change and reach new levels of accomplishment. Coaching is a life-line out of the muck, a new chance to experience personal success, and is highly valued and appreciated.

> **Unique.** Each coaching intervention is based on a unique set of circumstances and issues and requires a tailor-made approach for success.

A good coach is a partner in change, and must be willing to listen, tell the truth, and point out unseen obstacles or opportunities along the way. A good coach must be someone who knows the lay of the land — someone who has been there and mastered change himself. A good coach is someone who knows how to facilitate, give appropriate feedback, clarify, and motivate, all the while creating buy-in from the manager.

Management development coaching is about change, and is more powerful than most other improvement interventions. While not a panacea, one-on-one coaching goes a long way to enhance working relationships and bring about higher levels of performance, reduce stress, and increase employee motivation. And, while coaching directly affects the individual and his or her team, it indirectly ripples positive change throughout the organization.

There is no doubt that improving such things as role clarity, team communication and effectiveness, and management communication and support of employees can positively affect productivity and the bottom line. Changing the organizational culture from blame and criticism to one of acknowledgement and positive support are powerful adjustments that reduce stress and increase job satisfaction.

3. Increasing Team Spirit

With ever-increasing pressure being placed on employee productivity, including fewer workers to get the job done, less time to do it, and fewer financial resources, workers sometimes experience stress of a new kind: *spirit deprivation*. The unwavering focus on bottom line results, without a lot of genuine celebration, social acknowledgment, and rewards, has brought an emptiness that finds expression in troubling ways: like less commitment to excellence, and less team spirit to achieve lofty goals, and lots of high-cost stress. And with constant technology changes that keep us glued to our computers, the problem is exacerbated: less caring, less service, less concern for each individual's well-being.

There are some things that are clearly solvable, however, to reverse this trend and bring spirit back into the workplace. And the first step is to acknowledge the emptiness of joyful spirit that exists in the workplace. Which is not difficult to figure out. The first step typically includes assessing the current situation to determine where and how to focus attention. A great step that involves the team is to gather some confidential information from team members and then facilitate a meeting of all involved to discuss what's going on. This mini intervention elicits a great deal of energy and enthusiasm simply because it acknowledges each member as an important part of the team. The meeting will evoke some great ideas and suggestions to make changes. It's important to acknowledge that the manager has the final say and authority to implement the best ideas, as he or she determines are best. The bottom line, however, is that the participation and involvement of employees raises team spirit and greatly reduces stress in the workplace.

From a base of intending and creating greater team spirit there are additional steps to take in creating and carrying out an optimum plan for your teams experiencing stress-induced "spirit deprivation." For example, you might take the initial meeting forward by implementing strategic planning sessions to identify a new vision, implement lessons learned, shift team paradigms, clarify roles, and develop prioritized goals from which you gain consensus and agreement. And, finally, when you establish a culture of accountability and review monthly goals and responsibilities, it becomes easier to stay on track and achieve what you set out to do.

The end result? You gain Team Spirit that is …

S oulful in nature
P urpose oriented
I nspired and enthusiastic
R esulting in enthusiasm, motivation, and productivity
I ntentionally collaborative
T eeming with energy and excitement!

4. Guiding Employees into the Right Job Fit

There are certain key conditions for organizations to acknowledge and practice in order to be successful. One of these conditions is to **create inspired workers who have the necessary resources and information, who are in the right job, with the right skills, to produce high-quality work and be successful.**

This key principle of success reminds us that it's often useful to start at the end and work backward. Begin with: *"What are the desired outcomes?"; "What skills and abilities are needed to get the job done (to the standards you have already set)?";* and *"What resources are needed to support the work process?"* Figure these out first, and then fill in the blanks.

Nothing is more critical to reaching your desired outcomes than having the right people in the right jobs. It's quite important to understand that employees themselves often do not know where they best fit. In all my work as a career coach, I find that starting with past successes and areas of unique contribution, followed by newly creating an inspired job objective (no matter how much experience an individual has), is always useful. Clarifying and defining right job fit is a dynamic which changes over time.

Organizations which provide internal career development resources to employees, enabling those employees to understand where they want to be and best fit (either within *or* outside the system), are ahead of the game. Most employees need to move and change, feel challenged, and take on greater responsibility. Supporting them in this process is good for the organization because it helps people get to where they are inspired, motivated to succeed, and can more fully contribute.

CHAPTER THREE
Solutions to High-Stress Employees Dragging Everyone Down

The High Cost of Stress

In addition to "external stressors" many individuals experience in the organization, we can cause mental stress to ourselves without being fully conscious of what we are doing. Due to personal fear and anxieties accumulated and repeated over time, we may not treat our physical bodies as well as we should. Therefore, many of us need fresh insight regarding our behaviors and the cost of eating less nutritious foods, remaining attached to habits like overeating, using substances to numb our fears, and watching too much television instead of going for a brisk walk.

To reduce or eliminate the personal or internal stressors that individuals bring to the job, workshops are most effective. Individuals need to understand how they cause stress to themselves and the ways to overcome those ingrained beliefs and habits that are the cause.

This lack of awareness can be addressed by offering cost-effective **Wellness Workshops** to employees that actually provide a Return on Investment (ROI). The cost per high risk employee weighs heavily on your bottom line. On average, your high-risk employee (5+ health risks), incurs an extra $3,321 in annual medical costs. Your high-risk employees are also 12.2% *less* productive than your low-risk employees (0-2 health risks). In addition, smokers cost you $4,430 per year in lost productivity wages due to missed days and time off from work. Decreased productivity, absenteeism, and high health care costs add up fast. If you are not addressing these high cost markers through your current wellness program, let us evaluate and guide your employees to better health and working stress-free.

Taking Personal Responsibility Requires Ongoing Support

While Wellness Workshops help a great deal in providing new awareness, change can only occur when we each take personal responsibility for making it happen. Because real change occurs over time, it truly helps to be supported and reminded of what actions will serve us best. Ongoing employee **Wellness Coaching** includes the coach providing strategies to overcome poor health habits, automated daily health-tip reminders, and encouragement to continue on the path of achieving those wellness goals set by the employee. **Personal Wellness Coaches** support us for keeping on track until we embed the positive changes to be healthier and more fully functioning, creative adults.

The Need for Employees to Become Resilient

Change is a constant in today's world, and organizations do need to be nimble and respond rapidly to changing consumer needs. We generally assume that the nature of change is a stressor in itself, but is it really? While we look at change (external influence) as causing individuals to feel uncomfortable due to leaving the known for the unknown, a person who is centered or well-balanced may not react as others would. The reason is that some people are more "resilient" and are able to adapt quickly to new methods or strategies. According to Wikipedia,

> *"Resilient individuals have, through time, developed coping techniques that allow them to effectively and relatively easily navigate around or through crises and adversity. In other words, people who demonstrate resilience are people with an optimistic attitude and positive emotionality and are, by practice, able to effectively balance negative emotions with positive ones."*

We can each become more resilient and change our relationship with conditions that might cause stress or fear to arise. But we need to go within to cause the awareness for the shift to occur. With greater awareness, necessary changes can be implemented after learning and practicing important principles and better understanding the nature of our own reactive mind. This is best accomplished in **Employee Resilience Workshops.** (These teaching cover materials presented in the next Chapter: The Origins of Stress from an Internal Perspective.)

For optimum change that reduces organizational cost and creates greater employee health and resilience, workshops and coaching are highly recommended to transform your organization from one of adequate performance into being highly productive by taking these initiatives to create a healthy, stress-free, and energized workforce.

The following chapters go into greater detail about the many causes and solutions to personal stress that may be useful in understanding the ways or topics that can be addressed in workshops. In order to be successful, however, the exact workshop design needs to be a collaborative effort of managers and the presenter, which is easily doable. While the workshop material can be drawn from the content of the remaining chapters, managers, being individuals who experience stress themselves, may find benefit in reading this material.

CHAPTER FOUR
The Origins of Stress from an Internal Perspective

The Basic Cause of Stress

An interesting metaphorical biblical story that applies here is the casting out of Adam and Eve from The Garden of Eden. What could be worse (more stressful or fearful) than having to leave a safe haven, one of perfect peace and joy, to find a way to survive in the world of separation from the Utopia from which you came? And yet we all do this when we depart from our mother's womb. The key point here is that we humans unconsciously see ourselves surviving in life separate from a state of Oneness that many believe is our natural heritage. The quest that many humans have is to return to the safety of Utopia and overcome that stressful feeling of separation, whether it is on earth or after death.

Most of us go about trying to find Utopia in a perfect relationship, job, bank account, new car, or whatever someone perceives is the answer to what he or she is seeking. This approach stems from looking outward to acquire something in the external world, or physical reality, that we think will bring us wholeness we desire. And sometimes when acquiring that outer condition, usually for brief periods, the individual feels happy. But when the initial boost fades away, it's on to the next thing.

The problem with this scenario is typically due to how we've been taught, or conditioned to thinking is the way to happiness. Most of us seek comfort and satisfaction by going after and getting what we think will give it to us. Those "things" we seek are in the circumstances, conditions, or physical objects outside ourselves that we think will lead to satisfaction are actually the cause of our suffering, or stress. That's because nothing outside ourselves lasts or can give us the inner peace we desire. And, as a result, we constantly do battle with stress.

The good news is that our perception of separation is only perception, not truth. The world we see stems primarily from a separate ego point of view, not the reality of a loving, care-free state of wholeness. So the question is this: *"Is it possible to achieve a stress-free life?"* The answer is *"Yes!"*

Past attempts to deal with stress have primarily been focused on relieving the symptoms of stress, but not the underlying cause. What I believe to be a better solution is to stop stress *before* it starts. That is, to make a shift in the mind in order to see differently and to experience ourselves as already whole and complete. Certainly the need to reduce stress after it has taken hold is still a valuable practice and needed before the mind has learned to become untroubled. That is, to rest in its natural state of peace, goodness, and happiness.

In its purest form, stress is the effect of a "troubled mind" — due to having made inaccurate assumptions in childhood and practiced limiting or negative (fear-based) beliefs, thereby causing the individual to lose clarity of his or her true self and primordial nature of well-being. The troubled mind is fearful because it has believed it is separate from its Source, (or Wholeness, Goodness, or Love, depending upon how you prefer to think of "Source energy"), and thereby has taken on the (ego) job of thinking it must find something outside of itself to feel better. That is, overcome the fear of separation. Yet whatever it finds is temporary, and the mind returns to suffering, only to be followed by another quest for happiness. But each time there comes the feeling of *"this isn't it,"* the anxiety that is created is felt as what we now call stress. The troubled mind has forgotten that Goodness, Confidence, and Well-being is its true nature and cannot be lost.

It's important to recognize that we haven't done anything "wrong" in using the approach of thinking happiness depends on things outside of us, because for eons this is how we humans have been taught to go about life. It's just that when we become aware of how this way of living causes us stress, we can then shift the way we think. In fact, it is the stress we feel that is a signal to "pivot" back into alignment of *well-being feeling-thinking.* So awareness is one important key to "waking up," as the mystics say, and coming to recognize the dilemma we find ourselves in. Just think of that dilemma merely as *contrast* to what it is you do want: inner peace, joy, and the freedom to fully express oneself.

The thought that entered our collective minds eons ago was the belief in separation due to thinking that because we exist as separate bodies we must be separate from others, and therefore *ourselves*! We have given the body temple dominion over our understanding that we are, in fact, not the body but rather the mind. We have a body that temporarily houses the mind; but in truth, the mind is free and always will be. Our job is merely to recognize this truth, and begin to turn the momentum around to know ourselves as a collective and loving whole from which we have never been separate.

Fear, or the feeling of suffering, unhappiness, and not being safe in the world, elicits a fight or flight response that "juices up our bodies" (adrenalin rush) enabling us to run away from the Saber-Tooth Tiger. This results in the physical release of cortisol for the purpose of running fast so the tiger can't eat us. Most of the time, however, there really is no tiger — just a phantom dream we knew as a child when seeing a strange shadow from bed in the middle of the night. Unfortunately, for us, that continual release of cortisol whenever we perceive a threat causes all sorts of health problems over time.

The question to ponder, however, is this: *"Is the perceived threat really real, or not?"* If you believe that our reality rests in the mind, as many wise metaphysical teachers tell us, and not the body, maybe we are already safe being aware of it. Maybe it is our belief in separation that causes the problem. And maybe it is our ego separation point of view that causes our stress challenge to perpetually surface throughout our lives.

Healing the Gap of Separation

Healing stress comes from letting go of the ego-only perspective and allowing Oneness to unfold in our conscious mind, and then into our hearts and emotions to be expressed in physical reality. An amazing and immediate path to oneness, interestingly enough, is to feel good — a moment in which no outside threat is perceived in the mind. Would that it were easy to sustain those feelings even when things looked bleak in the outside world. Yet some people are able to do this when they choose to act as **witnesses** to what is going on, and not to get attached to the feeling-thoughts of an anxious mind.

The most effective way to go about healing the gap of separation is through meditation, as expressed by the Buddhist Monk Thich Nhat Hanh:

> *"Meditation can help us embrace our worries, our fear, our anger; and that is very healing. We let our own natural capacity do the work."*

The power of meditation comes as we witness or observe, rather than engage the stream of thoughts that appear in our minds. This act of "watching" quiets the mind and actually enables the brain to reorganize itself by synchronizing neural pathways that create a harmonizing effect in our conscious mind.

Deciding to become a witness, however, isn't quite as easy as it sounds. For a long time I thought I was effective in doing it, only to later discover that I was repressing feelings as they arose. Then I went the other way and started experiencing whatever came up — fear, anger, worry, etc. — all leading to adding stress in my life. Eventually, after years of my commitment to finding inner peace that included much struggle, I was ultimately able to find a method that worked for me.

Witnessing is not about either repressing or being run by feelings, but rather engaging with a "watchful eye." That is, experiencing without becoming lost in the feeling. Feelings are generally the result of thoughts, and thoughts are meaningless until we give them meaning. So while it is useful to engage feelings, it is also useful to recognize them as an experience we first gave energy to with a thought. This might sound complicated, but after you "get it" and the lights go on, having feelings is like having thoughts. That is, they are like having an interesting experience. We need not get all wrapped up in allowing them to run our lives or trying to avoid them. A good perspective to remember is that *you can have feelings without them having you*!

The practice of meditative witnessing goes like this: If we were on the side of a road watching a train go by, we could imagine each box car being a thought. If we weren't careful, when we saw a really pretty box car come along we might want to jump in and let it take us for a ride to some destination unknown. As we practice meditation and gain control over our mind we can alternately say to ourselves, "That's a nice-looking box car" and let it go on its way without giving in to an impetuous desire. The practice of meditation enables us to learn how to become better observers of thoughts and not take the ride into an unruly mind that will only lead us back to stress.

When we are engulfed in thought or riding along in the "nice-looking box car," it is hard, or maybe impossible, to be present or mindful of what is happening around us. In effect, we are unknowingly *resisting* the flow of peace and well-being into our lives. As we relax in meditation while attuning to our breath, we are clearing the mind of *"thought clutter,"* which is the cause of resistance to the inflowing love of Goodness or Source energy.

Learning to Let Go

In order to regain a more healthy perspective of sanity, I finally had to **let go of control and trust that things are always working out for me**. I had to learn what it meant to *"Let Go and Let God"* — a phrase I heard forty years prior in a twelve-step meeting. Please feel free to take the word "God" out of the equation, a word that causes both innumerable positive and negative reactions, and for that reason I use the word "Source" in its place. The word "God," just as all words in and of themselves are meaningless until we give them meaning, really only stands for loving, supportive energy continually flowing through us. Maybe think of GOD as:

> **G**oodness and Loving Energy
> **O**f which I am an inseparable part
> **D**ownloaded and continually flowing through me

For me the word "Source" if far more satisfying. Just use whatever word best works for you.

When I was finally able to let go of control and trust that the Universe was a "friendly place," (as Einstein suggested we consider), I was able to more fully breathe. I no longer needed to anxiously hold my breath and be hypervigilant thinking that the "Boogey Man" was lurking just around the corner. I finally learned (am still learning) to take deep and longer breaths without the worry or fear of being made wrong, criticized for not being good enough, or getting poked with a hot stick in the eye. I finally learned (am still learning) to relax, to let go of resistance, and let the Universe give me a hand. Try it, you'll like it. Deep breath in on four heartbeats, then slow breath out on four heartbeats. Repeat. Then come back to it whenever you begin to feel uptight.

Meditation as a "Passive" Method of Prevention

Meditation is a powerful tool that both helps us deal with stress that has already occurred, and, as mentioned, helps to prevent stress from occurring. The reason for this is that meditation actually changes the brain. Many studies have proven this to be true, with the change being that of producing greater equanimity, clarity, and spaciousness from previously embedded thought structures. Additionally, meditation increases clarity and the experience of "spaciousness" in which we are able to see from a broader perspective.

But the real power of meditation is that it enables our natural selves (pure, loving energy) to rise into consciousness. The perspective we need to take regarding this is that we don't have to be "saved" from some condition, or achieve something we don't already have, but rather to know we are already whole and need do nothing to earn it.

With this in mind and knowing we are perfectly safe in the world (regardless of the appearances or the evening news), it becomes easier to rest in peace, harmony, and goodness. Our true, unalterable nature is well-being or *Basic Goodness* (a term coined by 20th century Tibetan Monk Chögyam Trungpa Rinpoche), which our ego mind often refuses to accept. To regain this awareness we do need courage and bravery to keep from falling back into the trap of the ego perspective of judgment and separation. When I find myself desperate to seek comfort or find myself complaining about my circumstances, rather than trying to get somewhere or change something I don't "have," I know I need to relax, let go, and enter into a meditative experience to regain a truer perspective.

If you already meditate you probably have been taught to focus on your breath as the object of attention, which makes concentration easier. But researchers have also found that when practicing *calm acceptance* during meditation, you will develop a brain that is more resilient to stress. And if you meditate while cultivating feelings of *love and compassion*, your brain will develop in such a way that you spontaneously feel more connected to others. (Excerpted from ***Your Brain on Meditation***, by Kelly McGonigal, www.mindful.org)

Although you and I cannot simply alter the nature of modern life, you and I can counteract the effects of stress by resting in the peace and tranquility of meditation. New developments in brain wave audio technology now help us effortlessly accelerate the benefits of meditation by directly feeding the brain different frequency states in each ear that don't occur in normal awake states. This is a method call "brain entrainment," referring to the brain's electrical response to rhythmic sensory stimulation, such as pulses of sound.

This practice of mindfulness cannot be overrated, for as we practice non-attachment to our thoughts (like lying on our backs and watching the clouds pass by), the results can be the healing of many physical and emotional conditions, as well as reducing our daily stress. And just as you really cannot be masterful at playing tennis if you practice only once a week for twenty minutes, so too does it take some kind of daily or periodic commitment to meditation, if only minimal, to turn your new mindfulness skill into a habit. But there's a huge payoff. Wouldn't it be nice to enjoy stress-free living that enables you to be far less reactive to what is occurring and far more response-able to deal with any situation that arises? Your state of mind is the key.

The Return to Wholeness

Stepping back from our "monkey mind" enables us to more deeply experience Wholeness, Joy, and Peace to occur naturally on its own. (A wonderful "side effect" can include physical healing that naturally happens as well.) Our job, as individual minds not yet fully aware that all minds are an aspect of the One Greater Mind, is to practice meditation. Typically, however, our monkey mind wants no part of. But just ask yourself, *"Who is in charge here?"*, and allow your Personal Power that is always in alignment with Wholeness to give you the answer. As we let go of control and merge our seemingly individual mind into the greater whole, healing occurs naturally.

We have a wonderful guidance system already in place that can steer us in the right direction — back to feeling whole — if we correctly respond to it. That guidance system is our emotions, or how we feel in any moment. When we "fight" with current reality and try to force change to occur, we separate ourselves from the natural alignment with the Goodness of Source energy flowing our way. Uncomfortable, negative, or unpleasant emotions are an indication that we are off track. That is, we are engaging thoughts or reacting to beliefs that draw us further into separation consciousness and away from *who-we-truly-are* as a spark of divine love and innocence from which we have emanated and remain an eternal part of.

The trigger of any emotional distress is our cue to step back, see what's going on (what angst we are feeling as a result of not being in alignment), and pivot back to feeling good. Simple! But maybe not so simple to do, as it may initially feel strange or ridiculous that healing is that simple. What feeling good does is to realign us with the nature of who we are as a part of a greater Mind; that is, bring us back to ourselves.

Truthfully speaking, I have had a difficult time in exchanging sad or disappointed feelings with positive ones. The "trick," I found, is to imagine a future scenario that I want, and feel the effect of experiencing it. For example, if my bank account was low and I was experiencing stress, I would imagine how I would *feel* when having a boatload of money. I would relish the opportunity to travel more, experience greater freedom, and be more creative in expressing myself, etc. Imagining wonderful feelings is not the same as trying to control our mind to "think positively," and it is key to transforming our habitual patterns of negativity and worry.

You might wonder if the "boatload of money" arrives at your doorstep or comes flying in the window. It does not; but it is a good time to practice patience. Patience until you feel the impulse to take action. The flow of insight into your mind lets you know that the Universe has lined up some possibilities for you to respond to. It is your job to become the instrument through which Source energy manifests in physical reality *through you,* that is, through your actions.

The important point to know about practicing this (or other pivoting techniques — such as the ones I teach in my workshops), is that life evolves from that which we mentally and emotionally create. If nothing within our mind changes, the power of momentum keeps us heading in the same direction. Our job is to interrupt momentum that has us going down a dead end road leading to some kind of suffering, and redirect our thoughts and feelings to establish new momentum in a different direction.

In summary, it is only our belief in separation — to which we have been conditioned to think is real — that results in our feeling fearful and stressful. From that perspective we experience life being filled with worry and struggle. So here's the bottom line: if you feel bad, pivot to imagining feeling good. And the practice of meditation and witnessing will better enable you to do that. The healing that results will start a new flow of energy enabling you to re-align with your natural state of Wholeness and experience life as stress-free, joyful, and good.

Overcoming Vibrational Patterning

To set the stage, understand that all life is energy, and all energy vibrates at a particular frequency. Therefore we all project measurable energetic frequencies or vibrations all the time — whether we know it or not. Now combine this understanding with the law of quantum physics that simply states "like attracts like." According to Anne Taylor, Cleveland-based author of *Quantum Success*, *"We project energy in our emotions, beliefs, and thoughts, and that is really the source of what and who we attract [back in our lives], and is the basis of our sense of well-being."* Luminaries such as Plato, Leonardo da Vinci, Galileo, Beethoven, and Einstein all concurred with this understanding that is now referred to the Law of Attraction.

What is very interesting about vibrational patterning is that, without interrupting the pattern, it will serve to attract a similar vibrational response. Simply stated, if a person is angry and does not heal that condition, he or she will come face-to-face with angry people and not understand why that is. By the same token, if you wonder why someone who has five marriages all ending in divorce due to the same complaints of his or her partner, the reason is that the individual's vibrational patterning has gone on unchecked and the same kind of partner with the same kind of complaints keeps coming back again and again. I speak from experience here, as I have had two marriages and one long-term relationship by attracting the same behavior patterns in the spouses I attracted into my relationship. It wasn't until I figured this out that I began to change my patterning.

In addition to practicing meditation by witnessing so as to not get hooked by a thought, so too can you practice *not* responding with a knee-jerk reaction to things you thought were necessary to do. For example, when the telephone rings, it is my habit (coupled with an anxious response) to quickly answer it. All I feel is the adrenaline rush to "pick it up before it stops ringing." My anxiety is that if I don't answer it I will miss something important. In our modern day culture this addictive reaction is being referred to as "FOMO" — or the **F**ear **o**f **M**issing **O**ut! This vibrational patterning of mine has also caused me to anxiously be in a hurry so I don't miss anything important, and to check email messages way too often.

It took me awhile, but I eventually learned it was quite acceptable to "let the telephone ring!" In the meantime, I had become like one of Pavlov's dogs that would salivate at the ring of a bell because it had become conditioned to being fed immediately afterward. The dogs in the experiment would continue to salivate for some time after hearing the bell ring, even after the feeding had stopped. While picking up the phone would not lead to any food being delivered to me, nonetheless I had become conditioned to think it was absolutely critical to answer it. It took me a number of days to break this habit, which I celebrated by fixing myself a bowl of ice cream! (I hope I can soon break this habit as well!)

Years ago I was being trained as a Navy pilot, and in the early stages of flight training we practiced making many landings (a critical aspect for flying a plane). The difference in these landings was that we never fully came to a stop, but just touched down and took off again to circle around in the landing pattern for many more "touch and gos." This is also a useful metaphor (like "let the telephone ring") to consider as soon as you become aware of being hooked by a belief (a thought habit practiced over time) or a feeling (knee-jerk) response to a given situation. Just notice your action-response and "take off" again leaving it in the past to fade away. Notice the "touch down," then go!

The thing to know about this is that there is never anyone, including ourselves, to blame for the condition we find ourselves in. We get back into our lives exactly the kind of experience we are creating with whatever energy frequency we are emitting. Ultimately we are totally responsible for our lives, and experience the effect of whatever we are causing to ourselves. Which, when you think about it, is very good news. Because if we don't like our circumstance we can always change it. Not by trying to move around physical things or circumstances external to us, but by becoming aware of how we are creating our experience from within with our thoughts, feelings, and beliefs on the inside, and make a vibrational shift to attract new circumstances.

The "short answer" for how to begin a vibrational shift is to consciously change how you feel and think. The reason for doing this is because when our minds are all tangled up in a knot we will continue to spin around at the same low-level vibrational frequency — unless we interrupt the process and clear our mind with good feelings leading to higher energetic vibration. Continue the process by releasing ego-generated resistance to the flow of Source energy continually coming your way, which always feels good.

This is where all real change needs to first occur in order to raise your vibration and allow the inflowing and loving Universal energy of goodness to guide and carry you along through the process. It is not to say you needn't be responsible for your thoughts or feelings responses — for that is what makes up your energy vibration — it just means that you must become a co-creator with the same Source energy that created Universes. As you tune your frequency (like dialing in a particular FM radio station) to the same non-physical Source energy vibration within you, you access great power and ability to achieve the outcomes you desire.

CHAPTER FIVE
Additional Alternatives for Creating a
Stress-Free Organization

Stress Management Initiatives

A lot of stress management teachings suggest ways to deal with stress that are very useful. It is just important to understand that these techniques come after the fact — once we are feeling anxiety. What I have been suggesting is that we pre-empt stress by taking away the causes, and yet learning the stress-reduction techniques can be quite powerful in helping us regain our equanimity. In addition to the typical ones of getting physical exercise, eating well, loving ourselves, and meditation, one that also comes in quite handy is employing the Emotional Freedom Technique. EFT, or "tapping," is a way to release stress by acknowledging the unwanted feelings and tapping on certain meridian points on the body while releasing the negative feelings. This process then opens the door to insert positive affirmations for what it is we want to create in our experience.

But let's get back to some strategies to preempt the *causes* of stress. If we could remain in a pure state of *Presence* in which we give up the dream that *separation* is reality, and instead choose to align our energy (*who-we-really-are*) with the Source of creation and experience Oneness, there would be no stress. But not really probable, don't you agree? Well, except maybe for a monk on the mountaintop who meditates 16 hours a day and has no outer stimulation. But that's not us. So what to do?

Preempting Stress Before it Takes Hold

Most people seem to take life as it comes. Circumstances appear and appropriate decisions are made to make the best of the situation. If things don't improve, frustration builds and stress appears. There is an alternative to this outer-to-inner orientation to life, which is to become a "conscious co-creator" — one who uses an inner-to outer orientation to create or *manifest* desires.

By first starting to make the creative change in the mind rather than trying the change the outer condition, the thought-feeling vibrational energy starts the ball rolling. As the "rocket of desire is launched" (terms used by Abraham-Hicks) is released into the non-physical, what comes back to us are ideas, insights, and intuitive impulses that are consistent with what we put out.

To be a powerful co-creator means staying focused on the end goal and fully aligned with how it will *feel* to have achieved it. Then, as we take consistent action, unaffected by unconscious limiting beliefs, results take form. Important, as well, is that we remain connected to present moment goodness, or *Presence*, and remain unaffected by "monkey mind thinking" that can pull us off track.

Be Your Own Solution to Overwhelm

The solution to dealing with stress caused by overwhelm has little to do with "doing," but a whole lot to do with who you are BE-ing and how you are thinking. A ton of email, complex information, and projects trigger overwhelm, but they're not the cause. In all actuality, *you* are the cause. That is, part of who you are in times of stress like these might be called "Overwhelmed Janet" or "Overwhelmed Bill."

When those triggers happen, "Overwhelmed You" goes into full overwhelm mode. You feel stressed, confused, panicked. Your heart rate goes up and blood supply goes to your limbs for the "fight or flight" reaction. You're not thinking too clearly. You want to run away, grab some chocolate, drink a glass of wine, or, better, go to sleep.

Overwhelm is simply a reaction that is protecting you from a perceived danger triggered by all that stuff on your desk, in your email box, and on your to do list. All that stuff's not out to get you, but it seems like it! While it is possible to live in an almost a constant state of overwhelm, if we fail to manage it correctly productivity plummets, creativity ceases, and your work stops being fun.

The best response we usually have to overwhelm is to get organized. And there's nothing wrong with that, except that all you are doing is temporarily removing the triggers. But triggers have the habit of popping up again. You face 100 emails one morning and overwhelm is looming large again, bigger than life.

So, is there an ultimate solution to overwhelm? Yes. It goes like this: don't focus primarily on the triggers, but on connecting with another, different You. Let's call this "Focused You." Focused You is more resourceful, more calm, more present, more balanced. You have the skills and the ability to act from Focused You whenever you want. It's just that you forgot. Overwhelmed You took over and reigns supreme much of the time.

While the fear caused by overwhelm can seem like the Saber-Tooth Tiger with open jaws that stimulates adrenaline and a stress response, taking on the persona of the Focused You is your defense and wipes fear away. If the purpose of Overwhelmed You is to keep you safe from harm, then the purpose of Focused You is to act with clarity and intelligence. Focused You is interested in getting the job done, making a contribution, even doing what you appear to be resisting.

You might think of Overwhelmed You as operating from the edge of a storm, spinning fast; and Focused You centered in the eye of the storm — calm, clear, and peaceful.

To eliminate stress, reconnect with Focused You by first hitting "pause" on your "hurry-up-button." Then take a few deep breaths, and give yourself permission to feel the overwhelm, release it, and remind yourself that *you* have the authority to think, say, and do from a place of peace, wholeness, and clarity. A moment or two of silence followed by a powerful affirmation to reconnect you with your "center" can quickly turn the tables. The key is to first disconnect from your mind chatter and become present to your Wiser Self in the present moment.

When you step into Focused You, even in a chaotic situation with a lot of overwhelm triggers, you can still be calm and centered. Then you can more effectively make your priority list, handle your email, and get on with the important work that is calling to you.

Discernment Needed

To become stress-free, it's critical to discern truth from fiction. Just as the Saber-Tooth Tiger is now a phantom in our imagination, so too is a lot of stuff we make up. Maybe even thinking that the boss is now the tiger!

A big cause for "confusion-stress" is that we sometimes take things personally. Like, *"I'm probably the one to blame for things not working out."* Self-blame is a big stressor. Sure, we all make mistakes, but that's not a reason to self-criticize. We just need to embrace the feeling, learn from the experience, and charge back into life! And when we do charge back we need to remember to take the past-future concern out of the picture and be fully present in the *now* moment in which there is no stress.

So ask yourself, "Do you make problems personal to you, or do you take them personally?" Here's a quote from Eckhart Tolle to help clear this up: *"When you realize it's not personal, there is no longer a compulsion to react as if it were"* ... to which I add, and not become stressed out! Additionally, Don Miguel Ruiz, a Mexican author of Toltec spiritualist texts including his book *The Four Agreements*, suggests *"Don't Take Anything Personally"* (Agreement #2).

Another great "discernment teaching" of Don Miguel's is *"Don't Make Assumptions"* (Agreement #3). As you begin to give up the illusion of making yourself wrong along with illusions based on what you thought was true rather than actual fact, you'll notice a great deal more happiness and serenity flood into your experience. Remember to stay connected to truth in order to avoid "confusion-stress!"

Three Key Principles for Defeating Stress

There are powerful ways to manage thought-based stress and preempt the worry thoughts that might enter your mind. Here are three **Key Principles** I encourage my clients to implement followed by additional **Techniques** to defeat stress before it takes hold:

1.   **Accept.** First and foremost is to accept yourself, just the way you are. Maybe even make a vow with yourself (as I have done) to not criticize yourself any longer. And instead, to *love yourself just the way you are!* Then move from yourself to the outer world by allowing whatever the present moment brings to be OK. Simply stated, stress is caused by resisting what is occurring or what shows up., and you never win. As Byron Katie states, *"If you argue with current reality you will only be wrong 100% of the time."* So instead of fighting with reality, become a witness to what is occurring, get curious about it, and see what you can learn from it.

2.   *Claim Your Uniqueness*. Consider life a process that is unfolding only as it can for you alone. You are unique, so no need to compare yourself with anyone else, because they are unique as well. With this unfolding nature of your life consider and affirm that *"everything is working out for me in perfect timing."* And one thing many of us have been conditioned to believe is that we need to *be the best*. One notion to take worry out of this equation is to *"strive to be ordinary,"* and watch stress disappear.

3.   *Take One Step at a Time.* We call life a journey for good reason. On any journey there is a next step to take. As life is unfolding in perfect timing, be sure to remember that what you want — and will ultimately achieve — happens one step at a time. If you find yourself racing around and trying to achieve too much too fast, say to yourself **"stepping stones"** as a way to remember to slow down and remain mindfully in the present moment.

Eight Techniques for Defeating Stress:

In addition to employing the strategy of using the three Key Principles mentioned above, there are additional **techniques** for actually defeating stress before it can take hold. Here are my top eight:

1. *Gain Awareness*. If you find yourself getting anxious (which for me was trying to make things "perfect"), *interrupt* the thought-feeling response by taking three slow breaths. Next, give yourself a pat on the back for being able to do this! Then ask, *"What is going on? Is it really so important?"* The more you are able to check out and acknowledge what's going on, the more you are able to take charge of your mind and manage your thoughts.

2. *Practice **Being Content**.* If you typically find yourself wanting something different than what you have, you are most likely comparing the ideal to your current reality. This alone causes stress, so insert the notion that you would *prefer* to have something better, but you can get along just fine with what you have. Allowing whatever you have to be OK can begin to produce *contentment*, which may lead to **gratitude**. Appreciation is energy that actually opens the door for more good to come your way. So if you catch yourself complaining about what is, flip it upside down and be content with what is. And as you feel more and more grateful, your stress will diminish.

3. *Be Yourself.* Use your new-found technique of **Awareness** to catch yourself comparing yourself with anyone else. There is no one like you in the Universe. You have a special assignment, which may be as simple as making flower arrangements (because you love it and are good at it) that make people smile and feel happy. Your current situation is perfect for you right now, albeit one that is unfolding to your greater good. It's easy to say "love yourself" and harder to do, so just give yourself a pat on the back a few times each day and let that put a smile on your face and contentment in your heart. Forget trying to raise your self-esteem (which is solely achievement based) and go for **self-worth** instead — by acknowledging your basic goodness that is already dwelling within you.

4. *Rise Above Your Problem*. Look directly at whatever is bothering you squarely in the eye, then whatever image it produces, place it on the ground beneath your feet. *"Say what?"* Yes, beneath your feet so that you are walking on top of it! You are now "top dog" and are walking all over your problem and can handle anything that comes your way! In other words, while a

problem or challenge is present don't let it be the boss of your feelings. You can have a problem without the problem having you. Just notice the situation, "rise above it," and respond with *"I can handle this!"* Then go figure out how to do it.

5. *Ask for Help*. Honor the energy that created you, the world, and the universe as one of Wholeness. In fact, you cannot be anything other than connected with this all-powerful loving energy, and are free to tap into it and ask for assistance at any time — knowing it will be given — and typically provided in the form of inspired ideas to resolve whatever anxiety or concern you may have.

6. *Flip Your Limiting Beliefs Upside Down!* We all have beliefs — some that serve us and some that are based on confused interpretations from the past. Check out which ones seem to run you most of the time, or which ones stop you from taking action in the face of an unknown. Whatever the belief, know that you can never fail at doing anything. Yes, you can make mistakes, learn from the experience, and gain new knowledge ... but never *fail*. So if you come across a belief that keeps hammering you, or a critical voice saying you are unworthy, "not good enough," or a failure, look sternly at the message and turn it upside down. Recognize and claim the opposite. Then think it, feel it, and say it out loud. You are the master of your ship, so take hold of the steering wheel and turn it in the direction of your power and goodness. (Note: I address this area in more detail by having included a whole section on *Changing Beliefs* in the next chapter.)

7. *Claim How You Want To BE, and Trust That It Will Occur*. This is maybe the most important of the keys. When you wake up every morning immediately say to yourself ten "I ams" — slowly and with feeling. Like, *"I am wonderful, I am wise, I am worthy, I am stress-free, I am powerful, I am happy, I am abundant, I am healthy, I am content, I am skillful, I am loved."* Do this first thing before any negative or worry momentum begins. As the qualities you claim begin to take hold and you gain the faith to believe them as true, you will

see the "fruits of your labor" appear to a greater and greater extent.

8. ***Stay Present in Each Moment.*** Days and weeks and months and years are made up of tiny moments of happiness along the way. Thinking ahead can actually be the cause of stress. I remember this truism as a quote from Abraham that I think about quite often: *"A happy life is just a string of happy moments. But most people don't allow the happy moment, because they're so busy trying to get a happy life."*

CHAPTER SIX
Releasing the Past

Dropping Your Baggage

External complexity and communication overload that many of us experience daily just heightens our inability to accurately process the information we receive. Our list of stressors is so long in the modern world that our bodies rarely get an opportunity to stop producing stress hormones which leaves us in a state of perpetual fight or flight mode — the cause of all sorts of health problems.

Our "baggage" from past conditioning — the negative and limiting beliefs we store from the past in our subconscious minds fuel our responses to life. While some beliefs we have stored do serve us, many are critical in nature. This baggage lowers our ability to understand the truth about what's going on and lowers our ability to effectively respond to circumstance. The result of this baggage is having a "cluttered mind."

Too much stored baggage (through no fault of our own) reduces the amount of negativity we can perceive before we become over-burdened by stress. That level at which we stressfully react is called our **"threshold point."** The alternative to succumbing to negativity is being able to rise above stress, or become resilient in a way that overcomes the problem and allows us to experience our personal power never lost in our basic goodness and wholeness.

We all have different threshold levels and react sooner or later than others to the same situation depending on our ability to cope with what is occurring. Our personal threshold level is in some way related to having experienced fearful feelings in childhood and making up beliefs that turn into "habits of thinking" through which we perceive the world around us. These habits of thinking form the image of who we think we are in the world and affect our ability to be successful, earn money, and have positive relationships. While what we see may not in actuality be true, we believe it to be. And when we perceive the outer world not matching our inner beliefs about the way it should be, our stress hormones get activated.

Here's a personal example of mine to help clarify this. As a child I perceived my parents busy coping with life in the best way they knew how, and I felt unloved in the way I wanted or needed. As a result I made a decision based on an interpretation that those who were supposed to give you love were *unavailable* to care for me — and maybe even that I was guilty for causing it. Fast forward 25 years and I became attracted to a spouse who was ... you guessed it ... unavailable or unable to love me. Then comes a divorce, and we each went our separate ways, followed by a new attraction to a partner who acted quite similarly. I finally understood that changing partners is not the solution, but changing my beliefs about who I was *being* in the world — the way I perceived myself in relation to the outer world — is what was needed.

Many of us are limited in our ability to act with our full potential because we have attached to a belief that stops us in life. The belief we first set into place was a fear-filled reaction to make sense of and deal with a situation that confronted us, and maybe even challenged our survival in that moment. When confronted with similar situations we typically responded in the best way we knew how — with that same false interpretation which at the time made great sense.

By confronting and healing those beliefs that no longer serve us we grow our Personal Power. The more we feel our power the greater the ability to reduce stress and create a life of joy and full self-expression. Below are **8 Keys** to review prior to working the 10 steps that follow.

1. Limiting or negative beliefs originally began as false interpretations, and repeated over time became habits.
2. To "heal" or overcome a negative belief, now habit, requires ongoing practice. However, the 10-step process that follows will embolden your mind by guiding you in how to best *take charge of your thoughts.*

3. Thoughts are like race cars going around the track in our minds. We don't have the power to stop the race all together, but we can focus on one of the cars (thoughts) and call it into the pit for some service. When you notice one of your racing thoughts that creates stress, yell "Stop!" and tell it to pause for service.

4. Fighting with negative thinking does not work, but rather just serves to reinforce the existence of more negativity. So instead be a witness, watch, and allow the thought to quietly drift away from the track, ensuring it doesn't jump back into your race car!

5. The power to reframe your limiting beliefs was given to you by your Spiritual Source. You have the innate power to rule the universe of your mind.

6. Your Natural Self is the one that is connected to your Spiritual Source and Divine Goodness. By practicing "attunements" (meditation, prayer, Sacred Stillness, etc.) to your Source (or individual Soul) you develop a greater sense of your own goodness and have the ability to create a life filled with compassion and love.

7. By acting to help or serve the needs of others you take your mind off of the "me plan" and your upset rapidly diminishes.

8. When all else fails, turn your mind to gratitude, the great "mind shifter," and watch a feeling of goodness wash over you!

Changing Beliefs

Many of us are limited in our ability to act with our full potential because we have attached to a belief that stops us in life. The belief we first set into place was a fear-filled reaction to make sense of and deal with a situation that confronted us and challenged our survival in that moment. When confronted with similar situations, we typically responded in the best way we knew how — with that same false interpretation which at the time made great sense.

By confronting and healing those beliefs that do not serve us any longer, we grow our Personal Power to reduce stress and create a life of joy and full self-expression. Below are **7 Keys** to consider prior to working through a change process.

1. Limiting or negative beliefs originally began as false interpretations, and repeated over time became habits.
2. To heal or overcome a negative belief, now habit, requires on-going practice. However, the 10 step process that follows will embolden your mind by you *taking charge of your thoughts.*
3. Thoughts are like race cars going around the track in our mind. We don't have the power to stop the race all together, but we can focus on one of the cars (thoughts) and call it into the pit for some service. When you notice that racing thought, do yell "Stop!" and tell it to pause for service.
4. Fighting with negative thinking does not work. Your act of "aggression" just serves to reinforce the existence of more negativity. Rather, watch and allow the thought to quietly drift down the river (without you jumping on board!).
5. The power to reframe your limiting beliefs was given to you by your Spiritual Source. You have the innate power to rule the universe of your mind.
6. Your Natural Self is the one that is connected to your Spiritual Source and Divine Goodness. By practicing "attunements" (meditation, prayer, Stillness, etc.) to your Source (I call God) you develop a greater sense of your own goodness and have the ability to create a life filled with compassion and love.
7. By acting to help or serve the needs of others, you take your mind off of the "me plan" and your upset rapidly diminishes.

When all else fails, turn your mind to gratitude, the great "mind shifter," and watch a feeling of goodness wash over you!

Beliefs are the determinant factor in producing outcomes. Outcomes that we want and outcomes that we don't want. Yet the truth about beliefs is that they have no power. No power whatsoever, unless we think they do ... unless we *empower* them.

That's what we do or have done in the past and now are at the effect of. We have *"given authority to or have promoted the self-actualization of"* a thought.

Oftentimes the thought that we empowered was erroneous, one made in childhood when we had no reasoning ability to see right from wrong or truth from falsity. Yet these false beliefs have somehow taken up residency in our mind, continue to form the basis of our actions, and determine the outcomes in our lives. Isn't it now time to weed out these unwanted "rascals" and replace them with those we would rather choose?

Where are these beliefs? In what residence have they taken hold? How do they maintain such dominance in our lives if they were formed long ago? While it is generally believed that the negative or limiting beliefs we hold that create difficulties in our lives that we would rather not have, reside in our *unconscious mind.* That is, they are always lurking around ready to surface whenever the habit of thought brings them back up to the surface. Yet, if we can identify these beliefs, those such as *"I am unworthy, I am a failure, I'll never succeed,"* or an unwanted favorite of mine, *"money is the root of all evil,"* then they really aren't *unconscious,* are they?

There is no difficulty whatsoever in identifying these rascals. If you want to uncover any of your beliefs that don't support you in life, just look at and describe your current reality. Whatever experience you are having, just know that there is an underlying belief, positive or negative, that is at the root of your thinking. These beliefs are the basis of what you hold to be true and the actions you take that produce the outcomes in your life as they now appear. Do you see the consistency? Do you recognize that what you believe and hold to be "true" is how you then act? And in turn produces the outcomes that are consistent with your beliefs?

For many years I believed that my limiting beliefs held power over me, and that I was doomed to be at the effect of them. I tried to change them, force them to go away, and disregard them, but they persisted. Yet I could easily trace back to when I came to the conclusion I was "not good enough," etc., and even the exact incident in which they occurred. These beliefs held me captive, so to speak, until I found the way out. A way I hadn't considered or even knew about until I was referred to a book Maxwell Maltz, MD, entitled *Psycho-Cybernetics*.

Taking Charge

Before I give you the key points to unravel those beliefs that have (unconsciously) seemed to have control over your life, I suggest you try to clarify those beliefs so you can best relate to the process I suggested below. Here are five questions to ponder:

1. *What is the way your life is showing up that you don't want?* (Your outer experiences reflect the inner way you think and respond to life, and beliefs play a major part in creating those outcomes.)
2. *What are the beliefs you hold about yourself that are consistent with these results?* (Example: if you don't feel confident about taking risks, this suggests beliefs such as "I'm not worth" or "I need others' approval to survive," etc.)
3. Do you feel ill at ease around other people?
4. *Do you become anxious of fearful for no good reason in a situation that is relatively safe?*
5. *Do you believe that you live in a hostile or dangerous place?* Or just the opposite:
6. *Does success come easily?*
7. *Do you feel confident and like to charge forward into new opportunities?*

The beliefs you made up in childhood, between the ages of 0-7, basically had no relationship to the truth. They were just downloaded as software into your computer-type brain, and, as any good software program, just kept playing out repeatedly. Some assumptions were merely false interpretations based on the experiences you had. They were impressions, felt deeply, that you thought were true. Some impressions were quite positive, while others we not. These thoughts gained a hold and were repeated every time a similar situation appeared becoming a habit of thinking in a certain way. Eventually the habit was accepted as "the way things are." Let's call the negative or limiting habits of thinking "infantile beliefs" — childish, babyish, immature, and not reasonable, as one would consider as an adult.

Here are a few questions to reassess what beliefs work for you and those you want to change:

1. What is it about your life you want to change?
2. What might be the underlying belief that would support this outcome?
3. If you believed the opposite of this limiting belief how would you feel?
4. Now imagine you were free from this thought habit or belief about yourself. Now imagine feeling fully empowered to create the life you want.
   a. What would you be doing?
   b. How would your life be different?
   c. How would you BE in the world?

Key Principles for Eradicating Unwanted Beliefs

Below are **ten key principles for eradicating unwanted beliefs** and exchanging them for those you now choose, at this time in your life, as the basis of how you want to live your life going forward. Note that the action steps are not a one-time deal, as it is important to process back through, with emotion and commitment, in order to let your brain know you are back in charge, not the habits that have been living you up until now. As you withdraw the basis of anxiety in your life, you increase your well-being.

10 key principles for eradicating unwanted beliefs and manifesting your power:

1. Claim this truth: each of us is capable of exerting independence and knowing that there is something within that should not be allowed to suffer indignities.
2. Know that you have the talent and resources within you to be successful in any endeavor you choose and desire.
3. Look closely at your life by acknowledging the reality of your experiences.

4. Clarify and disregard any irrational beliefs from the past that don't serve you in the present moment. (For example, I once strongly believed I was inferior and unworthy, but whatever I undertook turned out really well. That is inconsistent.)

5. When you discover those beliefs that you have been giving power to in the past, rise up with anger or indignity about those foolish, immature thoughts.

6. Reject all foolish thoughts as "infantile folly." Dwell on the rational and throw out any inconsistencies or infantile thoughts that arise.

7. Acknowledge yourself for having taken back your power and taking charge of your life. This is important, for doing so will embed your power more deeply.

8. When you become overly preoccupied or give too much attention to your personal self, you can get buried in a trap of self-involvement. The antidote is to shift your attention to away from yourself and place it on what you want to manifest in life, your goals, or how you can be of service to others.

9. When it comes time to take action (based on impulses of enthusiasm or inspiration toward what you want to accomplish), ACT AS IF you will succeed given your worth, power, and abilities. Claim, with strong emotion, the feeling of already being successful.

10. Make use of the past only by taking what you learned and applying it to creating success. Mistakes are great learning experiences that provide the information you need to know to achieve success the next time around. (Avoid giving attention to the past mistake and focus instead on how to use the information in achieving your next goal.)

The next step is to clarify your strong desires supported by thoughts and feelings that will carry you into successful action. But first, claim the truth of who you are and shift the direction in which you go about living your life. Get into alignment with your true self, for that is where serenity and stress-free living is found.

Shifting Mental Habits to Live Stress-Free

As mentioned before, we react to circumstances based on our "threshold" — a point at which our underlying beliefs trigger stress. Everyone has a different threshold level, and some people react to situations with a great deal of fearful fight or flight response while others barely give it notice. As we clear up the negative underlying beliefs to which we have reacted to previously, our threshold level increases and we react with less stress to challenging life situations.

Some habits in which we previously responded to a situation are difficult to change. It is generally understood that to change a habit one needs to spend 21 days practicing a countering behavior to be successful. Obviously it's important that the commitment to change be strong enough to carry one through 21 days of mental behavioral change to be successful and not give in to the mind suggesting that *"it's not really that important."*

Let's say that you are now aware of certain underlying beliefs that have caused you to disengage from being happy, yet happiness still eludes you. Maybe now's the time to practice the **eight mental behaviors** listed below. In his book *Psycho Cybernetics,* Maxwell Maltz, M.D suggests it is a matter of consciously choosing *how to behave* rather than merely giving in to previous habits (like the way we put on or tie our shoes is something we do more or less unconsciously). Maltz encourages us to consciously decide and act in the following ways throughout the next 21 days:

1. *I will be as cheerful as possible.*
2. *I will try to feel and act a little more friendly toward myself and other people.*
3. *I am going to be a little less critical and a little more tolerant of other people, their faults, failings, and mistakes. I will place the best possible interpretation upon their actions.*
4. *Insofar as possible, I am going to act as if success was inevitable, and I already am the sort of personality I want to be. I will practice "acting like" and "feeling like" this new personality.*
5. *I will not let my own opinion color facts in a pessimistic or negative way.*
6. *I will practice smiling at least three times during the day.*

7. *Regardless of what happens, I will react as calmly and as intelligently as possible.*
8. *I will ignore completely and close my mind to all those pessimistic or negative "facts" which I can do nothing to change.*

Ten Steps to Turn Your Stress Habit Around

Try this ten-step turnaround process to reduce stress in the moment. When you catch yourself listening to a negative or unwanted thought that seems to have turned into a habit, turn it around to its opposite!

Name something or some situation you want but do not have. (How does this make you feel?)	What you now want:
Answer: *"Why don't you have it?"*	(Your answer often starts with the word "because")
Your "because statement" is your **limiting belief**	Example: "I'm not good enough" My limiting belief:
How do you feel when this thought comes up?	Feel it fully for a few minutes before releasing it ...
Check into the truth of your belief	In many situations when you look objectively at the facts, you will discover that your belief is not true! Or, the belief is merely an opinion that you added to the fact!
What are the facts?	Do they support or counter the belief you hold? Give specific examples here:
Enter a moment of *Quiet Reflection* and call upon your Spiritual Source to help release the negative belief	*Example in Buddhism*: notice your self-critical response (thought); forgive yourself, and reclaim your Basic Goodness.

Think of how powerful you would be it were impossible to attach to this belief!	How does this make you *feel*?
Choose a new belief consistent with this power, and repeat it often throughout the day	My affirmation to support my new way of being:
Breathe, acknowledge, and bring forth gratitude.	Take a few deep breaths and acknowledge your decision to take charge of your thoughts! Spend a moment in gratitude for whatever comes to mind.

CHAPTER SEVEN
The Need for Authenticity

Stay True to Being You

If you are not in alignment with *who-you-really-are*, your authenticity, you will automatically resist rather than fully engage in life. Resistance to anything causes suffering (or stress), and in this case anxiety from internally rejecting however life presents itself to you. Separation from one's true identity, having been trained to do life "backwards" (HAVE-DO-BE rather than BE-DO-HAVE explained below) creates the condition that we *not* be true to ourselves. As a result, we become a *"Conditioned Self"* rather than our *"Authentic Self."*

A powerful model to consider in overcoming these challenges and living an authentic life is this: BE-DO-HAVE. Note: this is the reverse of HAVE-DO-BE, or the way many people live their lives. Typically most of us have been programmed to believe that something outside ourselves is the key to happiness, which leads us to think that we need to "go get whatever that is" ("have") in order to be happy. Unfortunately, that kind of ego-based happiness is only temporary, for then we are on to getting more of the same.

Living in the domain of HAVE-DO-BE operates from one's ego orientation of feeling separate from his or her authentic soul-self. It is based on orienting one's life to the future or worrying about the past, and is based on a belief in lack, such as "I don't have what I need in order to be happy."

One caveat here. Life is rooted in the experience of expansion and change, and as we desire something and achieve it, we see there is more to desire in contrast to what we just manifested. There's never anything "wrong" about how we go about life; it's just that living solely from an ego perspective, without experiencing alignment with the loving force of non-physical energy (Soul, Spirit, Higher Self, etc.). our ability to more fully expand our consciousness and achieve a deeper sense of joy becomes limited. If we only go about trying to achieve desires by manipulating external objects and changing external conditions, chances are we will wind up unhappy. (There are stories of millionaires who are extremely unhappy after building an empire of wealth and choose suicide as a way to try and alleviate their psychic pain.)

The mirror opposite of only focusing on *having*, is this:

1. First, **BE** authentic — be true to yourself and connect to your heartfelt purpose.
2. Secondly, **DO** — as in share your gifts with others and make a difference.
3. And then HAVE, or receive the intended results you want in life, including abundance and everything else you desire.

The domain of "BE-ing," where it all begins, is about living in the present moment connected to the "Source energy" of creativity, goodness, and love flowing within and supporting you. A person who lives and expresses from the domain of Be-Do-Have typically holds a belief in abundance and trust, and is willing to become a Co-creator with Source while living in the present moment.

Here's the model below. Remember, go from left to right rather than right to left.

TRUST

Present Moment Orientation
(View based on Abundance Consciousness)

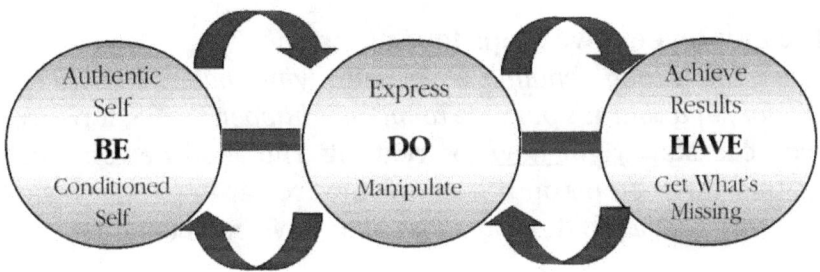

FEAR

Past or Future Orientation
(View based on Lack Consciousness)

Listen and Respond to Your Truth

When we listen to other people regarding what's best to do, we set up an approval mechanism by which we lessen our ability to take action that is right and best for us. This sets up a condition for lots of stress, for in always trying to find approval we never feel settled. Much better to listen intuitively to our heart-felt answers and, even though sometimes wrong, it is still preferred to unknowingly being led around by a "self-manipulated nose ring" all your life.

The manner in which we express who we are in the world is based on our self-image. The alternative to worrying about what others think of us is to gain a strong positive self-image in which we experience ourselves with confidence and dignity. With this being our state of consciousness we become far less a victim to stress than one who has low self-esteem. But the truth is we all have tremendous self-worth, but those with a poor self-image aren't aware of it. If we were all being true to ourselves and aware of our inner power and worth, feelings of stress would hardly be noticed. Our work, then, is to heal any negative view we hold of ourselves, connect to our voice of truth, and return to being authentic and powerful people we always were and are today.

Make Work Authentic for Happiness and Productivity

For the Employee: Two Steps for Success!
"Getting a job is tough enough ... are you saying that I can actually love my job, and that it's possible to make it happen?" YES, for sure! And you can start <u>right now</u> to create it. The good news is that taking this three-step route is more fun, rewarding, and easier than trying to get a job the way most of us have been taught.

Whatever you are thinking about your job, or how hard it is to find work, or how frustrating work is ... you are right. For whatever you hold as a belief tends to come about in the physical world. But the same is true for finding work you love. Only you might also have to engage this two-step process, outlined below, to achieve your dream.

Step One: *Discover the real truth about who you are*
The key here is that if you try to be someone you think you *should* be, or do *not really want* to be, or are not *gifted* enough to be, then no matter how hard you push you will never be fulfilled. The key word here is "be." Tune in and BE your natural self, first; then the rest of the process flows more easily. Other important words in addition to "natural self" are "authentic," "aligned," and "true." Find out that self which is true for you and aligned with your soul.

As a Career Coach for over twenty years I have found that most of my clients have trouble claiming or saying out loud exactly what their values, strengths, and passions are. In fact, just sharing with me their strengths is hard enough. So step one in the process is typically a self-discovery process in which the individual arrives at a deeper understanding of his or her strengths, passions, values, and life purpose.

Once you know what inspires you and what you are passionate about doing for true career/life fulfillment, you also need to see how your gifts can make a difference in the world. Life can become just mediocre if we are mostly self-involved in going after what we want; but it can also be joyous if you engage in contributing your gifts to others in need. A Career Coach can help you go through a process that culminates in a *Life Purpose Statement* from which you can base your actions. And with a deep commitment to your purpose, you can choose to stay on a course of action that might not be easy, comfortable, or filled with personal pleasure. But yet a course of action that is not only worthwhile and ultimately greatly rewarding — one that builds greater character, strength, and expresses your Personal Power.

Arriving at a Life Purpose Statement isn't exactly like pulling teeth, but it may very well be difficult. Why? Because we live in a conditioned culture where we may have come to believe that we are not good enough, skilled enough, or worthy enough to actually make a difference in the world and to manifest our dreams.

Step Two: *Manifest Your Dream Job!*
It is one thing to know who you are and what kind of work you want to have, how your aspirations can make a difference in contributing your strengths to others, and how to eliminate those beliefs that limit your full expression or stop you in life. Yet there is still a ways to go, which requires taking those actions that will lead to your intended destination.

And there may be more skills needed to pursue a successful job search, like what makes up exceptional marketing materials, how best to communicate your strengths with others, what goes into a good networking session, and how best to answer interview questions. It is hard to take all this on by yourself, which is why having a career coach might prove the difference between success and struggle. However, once these skills are learned and practiced and one becomes competent in applying them ***along with feeling confident***, then *"if it's going to be it's up to me,"* as the saying goes. True enough, but there's always help available along the way.

One way of moving forward, which I call "the old way" that has been around maybe forever, is to set a goal, determine the appropriate action steps, and charge ahead until the finish line is crossed. Kind of like a football team charging down the field only to be stopped by opposing forces. Seems like one could get roughed up or injured using this process, not to mention getting a concussion due to beating our head against the wall! Fortunately, however, there is another way that "manifests" the outcome we desire and side steps opposing forces.

Many teachers, coaches, writers, and thought leaders are using the term "manifest" because the process starts from within us, expresses outward, and combines with non-physical universal forces that are conspiring on our behalf. If this seems preposterous, know that it's actually no different than how Quantum Theory Mechanics explains the creative process. What happens next is this: from a committed and felt vision *as actually present in the now moment*, the Universe gets busy helping to orchestrate opportunities in your favor. New possibilities appear and inspired ideas lead to actions from which something delightful happens. Which may be what we want ... or not.

The BIG distinction is this: if what shows up is *not wanted,* it still must be embraced and let go — without frustration or upset. Then it is just back to the beginning without judgment: intention-vision-inspiration-action-result. Janet Atwood, NY Times Best Selling Author of *The Passion Test,* calls this process *Intention—Attention—No Tension,* which I think is a great way to think about accepting life — without fighting it — yet holding to that vision which inspires us as we persist toward our dream of rewarding and fulfilling work.

Manifesting your dream job is about claiming and being true to yourself, living in the moment, and letting go of trying to control life. And, additionally, opening up to and accepting the influence of non-physical loving forces combined with focusing on your vision, pivoting away from old beliefs that don't serve you, and taking action on inspired thoughts bring amazing results. I think this is the fun way to go, or at least should be. If the process begins to stress you out, check to see if there just might be a limiting belief you hold that is gumming up the works.

Above all else, have fun in your quest, and focus your attention on the positive and what is working. Claim success, however small.

And when you catch your mind starting to see the negative, thank it for sharing, but quickly return to what you are grateful for. Look through the eyes of appreciation rather than condemnation.

I say this not because it's a nice commentary on how to live life ... but rather because whatever you fill your mind with is what manifests. A grateful and positive mind, coupled with feelings of appreciation, actually attract good things coming your way. The Universe is always conspiring on your behalf, but needs a little encouragement and participation from you to keep the flow going and the good coming your way.

Connect to Your Heart to Achieve Real Success

Heartfelt expression begins by first aligning with the inner you, and then manifesting results in the outer world. Being your best is about being true to yourself in order to engage those around you with personal power, enthusiasm, and a clear focus on producing great outcomes.

Start with *who you are* and *who you want to become* by employing these **five secrets to living stress-free and achieving personal success.**

1. **Zero in on your *personal mission* in life in order to gain clarity of direction.**
   I have also described your mission as your *soul purpose*. In business it is often referred to as your *niche or your brand*. In career exploration your mission may include a combination of your strengths (skills plus interests) that define and support your job objective. In life you often hear that it's your *passion* that leads you to your dreams. Some others will say this is what you are "cut out to do." No matter the phrase or how it is described, it is something deeply unique within you that, when verbalized, expresses your authentic self in such a way as to "light your torch" and inspire others to describe you as the "go-to person" in that arena.

   You have probably thought of this one thing many times. You have probably been wanting to, or in part have been doing this in one thing in some fashion most of your life, yet you may still feel "off center" or not truly aligned with your purpose. If defining your mission or life purpose eludes you, think back. You might have been inspired by a book, a movie, a teacher, or a course in school, and said to yourself, *"That's what I want to do when I grow up."* And yet, that unique aspect of you may be more visible to others than it is to you.

This **secret number one** is identifying, followed by putting on paper exactly what your special brand, unique purpose, or authentic self is. This clarity leads to a focused direction. Then, as you truly own it and speak your inner truth to others, you gain tremendous power and influence.

Here is the thing about your personal mission: you are unique and have a special role to play in the game of life. When you accept that role, you are engaged in the game and offering your special attributes to others. And whatever it is you are here to give, to contribute, to offer to others, it's what they need to thrive in the world. So please don't hold back. You will also notice that when you are engaged in the flow of giving away your strengths you gain, rather than lose, personal power. Your strengths actually grow stronger. And very likely, when you are aligned with and "doing your purpose," you will lose track of time. You will be fully in the moment, and you will feel a strong force supporting you.

For many, the process of coming to know your unique purpose is a struggle. It took me about 15 years to fully get to where I needed to be. I kept getting closer, but was not really there until about five years ago. And as life is in constant flow and change, I deepen, evolve, and manifest my purpose to a greater degree all the time. So don't fret. Just go where your inner voice of wisdom directs. Take action, however small, on the one step just in front of you. Clarity will come; and as you pay attention and gain awareness, the direction in which you need to go will unfold.

2. **Learn from the past and develop the skills regarding what it takes to succeed.**

If you want to be the best leader you can be, I recommend growing your intuition, speaking, coaching, and relationship skills in addition to knowledge in your field of expertise. There's always more to learn. But don't overlook your own past.

Much of what we need to know going forward is what we can gather from past experience. A good exercise to do is to write down all your accomplishments, and then your disappointments for the past year or six months. Take a good hard look at both lists, and after patting yourself on the back for the achievements, ask yourself what you can learn as "takeaways." What are the important lessons that will be helpful to remember going forward? And then turn these lessons into three short, positive guidelines to post on your computer. Something like: *"Stay true to myself"* or *"Move forward through resistance"* (two of my guidelines for this annual plan year).

But lessons and guidelines alone are often not enough to get you to your desired destination.

I once used to think I did not need to further develop my skills. I thought I had all the skills necessary to succeed. But then I came upon some obstacles, some challenges that were new to me as I undertook a new venture along my pathway that is ever changing, growing, expanding. All of a sudden there were lots of things I did not know, and needed to know, in order to achieve the kind of success I wanted. So I went forward, almost as if I was being led by my inner voice, and started enrolling in those courses that would help me learn the skills and actions I needed to overcome my challenges.

Magic doesn't always show up on your doorstep. We all need to learn the "tricks of the trade" in order to turn what seems impossible into reality. Just like magicians, we need to learn, practice, and develop skills in order to pull our own rabbit out of the hat.

Going back to school for a course, either in a classroom or online, is a very good thing if it takes you in the direction of your dreams. Just make sure you know exactly the purpose of the course and what you need to get out of it before signing up. Then again, if you feel called to head in that direction, take action.

3. **Refine your Vision, formulate Intentions, develop your Strategy, and make a Plan.**
   Seems complicated, all these steps, but it isn't really. There is a flow to it. Visualize a cone. Into the top goes your vision, or what you chose (chocolate, vanilla, or strawberry, for instance) based on your desire. Intentions are next: they are your broad desires refined into personal commitments that you want and believe you can achieve.

   Critical point here: if you set up intentions without the belief you can succeed in achieving them, you probably won't. However, this does not mean you have to be absolutely sure of succeeding at doing the new thing you have never done before, but having the *feeling* that you can is all that is needed. Because inner creates the outer, start within. You may not know *how* you can achieve your intentions, and that's perfectly OK. The *how* will unfold as you go forward.

   A good strategy is also an imperative. You want to organize all the possibilities into a pattern and create a "structured approach." For example, if you decide to clean house and empty out the stuff that is taking up mental and physical space and which you aren't using, your intention is to collect and sell them, or donate those things to some organization or people who can re-use them. But before you start, you need what I often call a "structure for fulfillment." You need the boxes, the bags, the containers into which you can put all those things that you are letting go. When you finish collecting your boxes or getting the bags ready, you have a *strategy*, and an organized structure for success.

   Next comes the plan: when, where, and how the emptying out process actually moves forward. For complex intentions, or a vision that can't be handled in one afternoon, an initial plan to get started is what you need. Writing it down is a great way to keep it handy, refer it from time to time, score yourself on how well you accomplished the initial steps, then see what needs to be next. Maybe new ideas will come to mind to help you reach the target. And then make another plan! Each year I have an annual plan, and develop monthly goals, which I score and update with my coach, who assists me in staying accountable to myself. I am accountable to myself, not the coach, because it is *my* plan and not hers. She just happens to be an integral part to my staying on track.

4. **Take action on inspired ideas, and stay engaged.**

   Having a plan, a set of ideas that will lead to your desired outcome, is critical. And *sticking to your plan* is also of tremendous value, because constantly changing directions will just have you spinning in circles rather than manifesting your dream. The plan is a great support system to guide you toward the outcome you want.

   But here's the rub: your plan probably came out of a logical approach to getting you to where you want to go. But life does not always follow the logical path. At times, unexpected events occur, and creativity or spontaneity is called for. So step "lightly" — head down the road but be willing to check out new possibilities that come from inspired ideas in the moment. Maybe they will really help; and maybe not. If not, go back to the plan and keep heading down the road you are on.

   Achieving what you want is great. But missing the mark is far better than sitting on the couch wondering what could have happened. Life lessons are gifts; learning is one thing we're here to do. So take action, stay engaged, and carve out your statue from the huge block of marble you were given at birth. If you intended to carve out a beautiful goddess and came up with a bullfrog, great! You have an outcome and contributed to the world around you. And, who knows, maybe the next guy will find a way to kiss your bullfrog and turn it into the princess of your dreams!

5. **Work with a coach to become a master of managing your thoughts, creating results, and celebrating victories.**

The biggest challenge we have in life is dealing with our thoughts, conditioned responses, and made-up rules we learned as we went through life. The misinterpretations are not the problem, however, once you gain awareness about how your conditioned thoughts have caused you stress. It is merely the repetition of them that gets us in the rut we may be in.

How to get out of the rut? A coach, or someone to talk to for the purpose of sharing your limiting beliefs, is a great way to uncover the falsity of your thinking and replace it with new, empowered paradigms that help you better see and take action on what you need to do to achieve the results you want. We all need support and inspiration to succeed, so ask for it.

A coach can support you in not only gaining awareness of your making false evidence appear real (FEAR), but in your practicing and implementing new thinking and behaviors, over time, that get you out of the rut. New momentum heading in a new direction is what is required. Not unlike a car stuck in snow needs to rock back and forth to build momentum to escape the rut.

Here's an example of how a coach recently made a huge difference in my life. On a call, he pointed out and reminded me about the use of "Gold Time Management" (a technique we teach at Best Year Yet®). A light bulb went on when it occurred to me I had given my power over to and become a sort of slave to emails, phone calls, and dealing with the seemingly urgent stuff that was really not part of my priority goals. With that awareness I was able to get back in the driver's seat, take charge, and turn my focus on what was really important.

In addition to helping us manage our thoughts and demons and invalid assumptions we have made that seem real, a good coach is someone who can guide you in better understanding the "secrets of landing the life of your dreams." Find someone who can ask good questions, acknowledge your greatness, guide you in appropriate action taking, and partner with you in achieving the success you want.

CHAPTER EIGHT
Strategies for Dealing with Stress at Work

Neither the management of an organization nor the employees want to experience stress at work. Stress costs lots of money, reduces productivity, and creates lower morale and greater absenteeism. Change is not only possible but quite doable. It is time we all take charge of and reduce the factors that create a stress-free workplace in order to unleash greater organizational success.

Having addressed the external or structural factors that cause stress in organizations, it's important to focus on employee strategies as they arise in the workplace.

Become a Witness

The truth is that you can only move forward and develop your true potential in direct proportion to the amount of negative emotions you are willing to release. When you observe negative emotions and feelings consciously, without reacting to them, they eventually lose their power and fall away. Simply observe, don't get involved, don't try to stop the emotion. Just curiously observe where it is coming from. You will probably recognize these emotions by a feeling somewhere in your body. Just simply observe with curiosity like a child does when discovering something new and intriguing.

This is the same process you can use anytime you are at work or in any situation in which you first notice anxiety. The steps are these:

1. STOP (and take two or three slow deep breaths).
2. Gain awareness about the facts of what's going on.
3. Describe (to yourself) the outer situation.
4. Identify your inner response.
5. Fully breathe again and release negative emotions (as described above). Holding on to them is like driving a car with the emergency brake on.

6. Ask yourself: *Do I have to react in a fearful way, or can I just notice my reaction and watch it, knowing I cannot be harmed by anything other than my thoughts?*
7. Remind yourself that you are always whole and connected with inner peace, regardless of your feeling reaction in the moment, and whether or not you are consciously aware of it.
8. Connect to a positive feeling and choose an affirmation you can use to replace your reaction. Example: **"I am taking charge of my life by becoming an observer and not reacting. I am growing stronger and more resilient every day."**
9. Ask yourself, *"What's the truth in this situation?"* and make a request, if appropriate.
10. Shift gears, turn your attention to the future, and move on.

Don't Accept What Others Think of You

It is quite common for many of us to experience a stress response when communicating with an "adversary" — one with whom we are in a challenging relationship, has a different point of view, feels controlling or wanting to dominate, is demanding, or merely has a loud voice that invokes a memory of a dangerous situation. This behavior typically causes us to tighten up, withdraw, protect, or even want to vanish from the scene. But let's say this is our boss from whom we cannot run away from. What to do?

As in any stressful situation the first thing to do, as best we can, is soften up a bit so our mind becomes more clear and aware of what's going on. That is, breathe and let go of the tension. We need to get back to first reclaiming our identity, which always exists as perfect safety regardless of the situation. Then know that what people think of you, judge you, or decide they know the kind of person that you are is merely false thinking on their part. In actuality they have misidentified themselves as separate, and are coming from a place of fear (and projecting that onto you).

The next thing to know is the following, taken from a teaching of Abraham during a workshop in Asheville in September of 1998:

"You have more harmony points with every person on the planet than you have disharmony points, because there is much more of you that is in harmony with your Core than you realize or that most of you allow. The closer you come to being in harmony with your Source Energy, the more in harmony you are with each other.

When you think about other people and what they think of you, do you understand that what they think of you has very little to do with what you are? It has mostly to do with the habits of thought that they have developed. It has more to do with them as thinkers than it does with you as the subject of their thought."

Within us rests the truth of our being, one fully connected to Source energy of wholeness in which we experience no separation. The feeling of separation, however, can easily be felt as we layer on top of our true identity thoughts that separate us, limiting beliefs, old "vibrational patterning," and conditioned experiences in which we were sure the saber tooth tiger was about to eat us.

All that layering sets up a kind of false conditioning that separates us from oneness with ourselves and all other people we come in contact with. So the point is this:

Reduce Stress by discounting the effect of what other people think of you, how they react to you, or however they relate to you in any given moment. Reclaim your own connection to Source Energy and feel good, regardless of how the outer experience might have tended to influence you in the past. Remember, nothing other than your thoughts, beliefs, or feelings of being separate from Love can cause you to feel bad.

Become Aware of Your Misidentified Automatic Response

Automatic thought responses can cause all sorts of stress unless challenged with awareness and reason. When clearly seen for what they are, these errors in thinking can be countered with logic and rationality that can thereby reduce your stress response. Here are some examples of misidentified thought responses:*

1. **All or Nothing thinking** sees only two categories of possibilities, rather than possibilities existing on a continuum.
2. **Anticipating Negative Outcomes** is expecting whatever will occur will be bad by thinking the worst will happen or "predicting" it or without considering other alternatives.
3. **Discounting the Positive** occurs when you are telling yourself that the good things don't count. The opposite is also true when you believe that only the negative thing will occur based on one detail rather than the whole picture.
4. **When your emotional response** overrides the rational or logical response to the situation when you are sure that what you feel is true.
5. **Making Assumptions** based on what you believe others are thinking without checking it out.
6. **Perfectionistic thinking,** or making unrealistic expectations that have little chance of happening. (This response can then lead to feelings of guilt or upset due to missed expectations.)
7. **Self-Critical thinking,** believing you are at fault and condemning yourself unnecessarily.

The key point to member is that thoughts alone cannot hurt us. It is we who hurt and cause ourselves stress by believing untrue thoughts are true.

If or when you can come to believe that Wholeness and Goodness is what's true and that we each are unconditionally loved and innocent just as we are, it becomes easier to act with a "mindful heart." That is, noticing whatever occurs is merely an interesting perception, but not necessarily true, and then letting it pass. When we can learn to trust that *Life*, or *Source Energy*, is supporting us and to which we are always connected, life becomes much more joyful and stress free. And as we become more curious observers in life, rather than ego-based irrational thinkers, we can begin to let go of *Resistance* to the love and support that is always flowing our way.

(*For more information on this response to "false thinking," please refer to *Cognitive Therapy: Basics and Beyond* by Judith S. Beck.)

Turn Stress into Peace of Mind

(A portion of the content information below was adapted from a talk by Tara Brach, a well-known Buddhist teacher and Psychotherapist.)

One of the significant keys to living, growing and learning to abide in well-being is to continually gain awareness, or become mindful of what's going on in the moment. This is especially true when it comes to gaining clarity about challenging situations, including the origins and differences between stress, fear, and anxiety. For example, while we typically think that fear and anxiety are pretty much the same, in fact there is an important distinction between the two we need to be aware of. The reason being we need to respond differently to each.

To begin with, **Fear** is a response to an ***immediate*** perceived threat or danger. For example, someone pulling out a gun and pointing it at you. Or you see a small child about to go out into a busy street unaware of the traffic. The physiological response is similar to anxiety in that cortisol is released and the fight or flight response takes over. In this case it is very appropriate to take immediate action and try as best you can to diminish the threat in the moment.

In contrast, **Anxiety** is a biological reaction to the ***perception of a future*** threat to your well-being. While the threat is not actually occurring in the moment, the body responds as if it is, causing the same physiological reaction and fight or flight response.

The Need for Mindfulness

If we continue to allow ourselves to become the "victim" of our own mind making up anxious stories about the way things *might* turn out, we can actually start a habit of calling forth anxiety. And even worse, the habit can become chronic, even addictive, and more difficult to change.

Therefore, it is important to interrupt our reactive response to our mind creating fearful scenarios, take charge of our thoughts, and change our response in the present moment. However, once we have created anxiety, we can take a few steps to turn it around. Below is a **five step process to release anxiety once we have experienced it.** What's important to remember is that being more mindful in any moment can be the deciding factor in whether we experience stress or well-being.

1. Notice your discomfort and become mindful of your anxious thoughts as they arise.
2. Close your eyes and allow your feelings to "drop into your body" as you become mindful of your physical sensations occurring in a particular area of your body (versus trying to push the feeling away).
3. Offer a feeling of comfort to yourself as you release any negative energy.
4. Open your eyes and reconnect with the physical world (look around, listen to sounds, etc.) and to the present moment.
5. Notice the change within you and, if appropriate, give yourself a phrase to recall when anxiety begins to arise again (like *"I am always safe no matter what," "I can only be harmed by my thoughts," "In my defenseless my safety lies"*).

Transformation happens over time as you continue to practice this shift or "pivot" from thinking that a future danger can harm you in the moment to noticing, feeling, and letting go of anxiety. Staying mindful is key, as well as soothing yourself with comfort.

The Basis of Worry is Self-Doubt

Just as worrying can become a habit, so too can replacing worry occur over time. This requires gaining greater self-confidence and the feeling of self-worth that "displaces" the negative response due to self-doubt.

To lessen your anxious and reactive thoughts and feelings caused by worrying about a future scenario, practice acknowledging yourself more and honoring your achievements. Basically you need to "de-condition" your worry response by honoring the goodness of who you are as a dignified and confident human being.

Become More Courageous

What if you are in a job or work situation that doesn't fit with your true self? What to do? Here are eight that you may try out:
1. Notice your complaints and make requests to empower yourself. (Beneath every complaint is a request.)
2. Communicate with power: *"When you ___ (describe behavior)____, I feel _____. I would appreciate if you would _____. Is that doable?"*
3. Discuss with "possibility in mind" vs. "trying to get your way."
4. See yourself in a dodge ball game, and step out of the way when you are the target.
5. Develop unique affirmations, with feeling, and repeat, repeat, repeat.
6. Always do your best so you can get recognized for your contribution in order to have bigger "clout" when you make a request.
7. Take some risks that feel "right."
8. Talk to your boss about what you are good at and passionate about, and see if there are ways to do more of that which resonates with your true self.

Make Lots of Mistakes!

Most of try to avoid making mistakes, and for pretty good reasons. Like we want to succeed at what we are doing. Or maybe we think making mistakes will bring on stress. But actually just the opposite may be true!

The downside of trying too hard to get things right may mean that you aren't learning anything new. And trying to get things "perfect" can be really stressful, especially if you are worrying what others will think if you do make a mistake. For years I was burdened with "perfection thinking," much to my detriment, due to the added worries and fear it created. Basically I was stuck on the "hamster wheel of needing approval." Fortunately I started to see the folly in all that and dropped that habit.

The truth is that life can be "messy," and messing up can be very healthy! It means we are going forward, trying new things, engaging life. It means we are alive! When we stop and pull back, it means we are afraid, and fear is no way to live life. Courage is the name of the game.

Remember that making mistakes does not mean you have "failed" or, worse yet, you are a failure. It means you are OK and doing our best. When things don't go as planned just gather new information, make some adjustments, and get back in the game. Making mistakes means you are on your way to achieving your desired goal, just not quite there. But you are in action. You are fully alive.

Here's a quote I found recently, one by Neil Gaiman. So if you find yourself getting tied up in knots and becoming stressed by desperately trying to avoid mistakes, read this through again. It's called "Make Mistakes!"

> *"I hope that in this year to come, you make mistakes. Because if you are making mistakes, then you are making new things, trying new things, learning, living, pushing yourself, changing yourself, changing your world. You're doing things you've never done before, and more importantly, you're Doing Something.*
>
> *Make New Mistakes. Make glorious, amazing mistakes. Make mistakes nobody's ever made before. Don't freeze, don't stop, don't worry that it isn't good enough, or it isn't perfect, whatever it is: art, or love, or work or family or life. Whatever it is you're scared of doing, Do it."*

Ask for Help

If a roadblock gets in the way or you need assistance and someone else has what you need, **asking can be the powerful thing to do**. While it may feel a bit humbling, it does provide the other person the opportunity to contribute *to you*, which many of us want to do in life anyhow.

I have a friend who used to think she should and could do everything for herself. What that got her, unknowingly, was a struggle in relating to others. People tended to stay some distance away, as she was not open to being contributed to. Once she started to change that habit, she not only found others were more open and easier to relate to, but a great dancing partner who would travel halfway across the world to go dancing with her!

Asking for help is a sign of strength, not weakness. Asking can help acquire resources, gain opportunities, and make what seems impossible very doable. If your intention is worth pursuing, go for it, and ask for what you need.

An important point to remember is that others do not know what you need until you ask. Years ago I volunteered to head up a fundraising project for a non-profit organization called Hand to Hand, a small, one-of-a-kind organization committed to ending hunger on the planet. Enthusiastic, highly persuasive, and talented individuals ran the place, and offered training to those volunteers who were being asked to raise money for any number of organizations engaged in ending hunger. One Saturday I attended the training, and a light bulb went on.

At the time I considered myself a fairly persuasive person and able to speak passionately about what was important to me in life. In conversations I would banter with the best of them, trying to make my point as I upped the level of passion and enthusiasm I had for the subject. After a while the conversation would fade, people dispersed, and usually nothing much was accomplished and not much changed.

At the training, the Founder of Hand to Hand taught us that, while in many fundraising projects there were well meaning volunteers who could and did speak passionately about their cause, often not much money was raised. Charlie (the Founder) coached us on the most important part of the fundraising conversation which came *after* we spoke passionately about our cause: the part where we had to actually ask for a contribution!

At the time this bit of wisdom felt uncomfortable to me. Weren't people supposed to know what I wanted? Well, no, they don't. And I should not expect them to. Chances are the person or organization we might want something from is not going to pay us much attention. They are probably too busy or too wrapped up in their own world to even notice us.

The one downside to asking for help that stops many of us from making requests of others is fear of rejection. Anyone to whom we make a request is free to decline it. But the upside is well worth the risk, and the results that can come from receiving the assistance can be dramatic.

What to do with rejection? First of all, as we take on the risk of rejection and experience it a bit, the fear diminishes over time. So "stay in action" is a good mantra. Thank the person for considering the request, and move on to someone else. Not everyone is going to say no; be persistent and go find someone else who wants to and can contribute to your worthy intention. Just make your request knowing "no thank you" is one response you may receive. Including your boss.

A great example of asking for help is in seeking different work — including different work in the current organization. Just **ask** for a networking meeting. It's quite effective to say to one of your internal contacts, *"I would appreciate 20 minutes of your time to get your ideas and suggestions on how I make a more relevant contribution. Would you be willing to meet with me later this week"?*

By asking for and receiving help or assistance, you will create success in achieving what you want. And what might benefit others as well. Ask; it's the right thing to do!

What to Remember

Anxiety based stress is very rather common in today's fast-paced life and sometimes affects us. But we needn't accept it as reality, for we can always respond to it with mindful awareness.

In summary, if you want to enjoy life rather than feel caught in a web of stress and anxiety, begin by pivoting from future worry to present moment awareness. First, "drop" your consciousness from your head into your body and feel what your body is telling you. Then recall the truth: *"If I am feeling fearful about a future scenario, I must be mistaken for I am attacking my wholeness in a moment that doesn't exist! So instead I choose to let that false thought go, comfort myself as best I can, and turn my attention to the present moment of goodness in which I am a powerful and capable participant in the adventurous game of life!"*

A good Segway back to the moment and staying centered is to find something to be thankful for. *Feel appreciation* for whatever inspires you and honor yourself for having taken charge of your mind rather than letting it take its own course of false thinking. Then get inspired by something that you want and let your enthusiasm and intuition guide you into action taking action, knowing you are a co-creator in the game of life!

CHAPTER NINE
It's Up to YOU!

Create a Plan Before Making Change

I once asked my good friend and a therapist on the golf course a question that had been bugging me. I said, *"Dan, what is the best way to make change?"*

As Dan turned to head in another direction to his ball he responded with a single word: *"Start."* Hmmm ... how profound, I thought!

But before you jump in willy-nilly, it's good to step back, get a bigger perspective, and create a plan. Your plan needs to come from within you and be something you feel really good about. As my friend Marci Shimoff, *NY Times* bestselling author of *Happy for No Reason* says, have it arise from your *soul* rather than from your *ego*. To that end, here are a few Soul-inspired questions to guide your thinking before coming up with a plan.

1. How do you want your life to be six months from now?

2. How differently do you want to feel?

3. What needs to change in your current thinking?

4. What needs to change in your current behavior?

5. What have you learned from reading this book?

As a result of these questions, I suggest you develop a plan to embed new ways of being in the world to raise your energy level of feeling good most of the time. (Your feeling good is an energy vibration that attracts back similar good-feeling experiences.) Consider the following ten categories to incorporate into your plan, including ways you can:

1. Improve your physical and mental stress-free health (like starting a meditation practice, for instance)

2. How you can be and express more of your true self
3. How to handle stress in the moment it arises
4. Accepting who you are as a powerful person
5. What to do long term that aligns with your purpose
6. How to better work together with your colleagues
7. Ways to use more "I messages" at work and home
8. Help and serve others to feel more joyful
9. Remembering to say "thank you" often
10. Feel gratitude every day

Keep your plan simple, and initially tackle only a few changes you want to make. (No reason to put unnecessary stress on yourself, right!?) Maybe have it fit this kind of table:

Area I wish to target	Action to take	When to complete	Result to achieve
Example: Start the day with clarity and calm rather than feeling hassled	Meditate every morning for 15 minutes	Daily, before I go to work!	Greater peace of mind when the day gets hurried or overly complex

The key thing is to review your results, (whether once a week or once a month) to see how they line up with your desired outcome. After gaining some experience using the new behavior modify your strategy, as needed, going forward.

Be Determined to Succeed

Have you ever gotten to a place of momentary awareness that your life has been shaped by a belief that turned into a way of living that no longer serves you? I have. It happened again recently as I was listening to a webinar talk about something that was actually unrelated to my new 'ah-ha' awareness. I saw how my whole life evolved from this one decision that colored everything that happened after that, even though I was totally unaware of how I was shaping my own destiny with the paradigm I was holding as true.

The thing about these paradigms, in addition to our often being unaware of them, is that they are neither true nor false, but are acted out according to the power we give them. The key is to keep seeking new awareness that gives us the power to change. What a gift it is to come to clarity!

There was a prior event that happened a few days before my lightning strike of insight that added fuel to my interest in making a change. If you aren't aware of it, Tom Brady, the quarterback of the Patriots, is known for his ability to lead the team to victory in the 4th quarter when the team is behind. And sure enough, it looked like the Patriots would fall to the Giants once again. With just a little over a minute left on the clock and with eighty yards to go for a score, the Patriots were behind by 2 points. What I noticed was not just the plays that ensured, but the presence of Brady on the field. I actually felt that he was not only determined to win the game, but felt sure of it. He simply wasn't going to lose, and did not even appear to consider that possibility. And even with 4th down and 10 yards to go to keep the drive going, Brady hit his receiver for eleven yards. Miraculous, you might say. I say it could *not* have happened differently, given Brady's resolve.

So, the moral of this story is this: whatever happens is deeply affected by the thoughts and determination you hold relative to your underlying beliefs. If you feel like a victim in some circumstances, or undeserving in others, you attract those results. If you feel like a winner and a powerful creator, that's what you get. The point is this: no paradigm is best, or right, or wrong.

Beliefs just attract back the energy of the feeling-thought unconsciously expressed.

Is there a way to get clear about your underlying beliefs so you can change your thoughts and change your life? In part 'yes,' in part 'no.' The yes part can be found in a process I share in my new book, *The Joy of Living — Seven Steps to Give Up Worry, Open Your Heart, and Love Your Life,* now available on Amazon.

The 'no' part has to do with the combination of readiness along with the request for help to find your answer that your intuition or others are always ready to answer. Life is an unfolding journey that flows from experience, beliefs, lessons learned, insights, frustration, and, ultimately, success. And asking for help is a key ingredient to a successful outcome.

But that's life: the happy parts and the unhappy ones. But as one of my teachers says, *"Celebrate the unhappy parts (as well as the happy ones), for those are the ones that lead us to the desire for change and expansion."* Which is what living is all about.

Three Final Tips

Finally, I will end with three easy-to-remember suggestions.

1. Love yourself no matter what, wherever you are, or the skills you have in dealing with stress. Love is the most powerful healing energy, so use it often!

2. "Forgive" the stressful situation. That is, let it go without judgment, "rise above it," and return to the experience of *Presence* (a soulful connection to Wholeness and Love).

3. Treat others as you want to be treated — with kindness, compassion, and love. What you put out and how you perceive the world returns to you, many times over!

THE END

ABOUT THE AUTHOR
Jim Koehneke, MA
Business & Life Coach

As the Founder and Senior Coach of Love Your Work Today, a Business and Life Coaching business, Jim supports individuals and organizations in discovering and expressing clarity, power, and full life participation. He is an inquisitive life learner who is passionate about personal development and spiritual fulfillment, and loves teaching and coaching others how to awaken to their calling.

Prior to starting his own coaching and consulting business Jim served in key Human Resource Management positions in Education and Manufacturing before becoming a Senior Coach and Vice President of Client Services Consulting for an international career transition consulting firm. He has taught Professional Development courses at the University of North Carolina at Chapel Hill and Montgomery College in Rockville, MD, and served as an adjunct Instructor in a Master's Degree program teaching a Life Coaching class at Burlington College in VT.

Jim's first book, *Creating and Living Your Purpose*, helps individuals identify their unique purpose in life by using success strategies to create the work they love. Jim's second book, *Take Charge of Your Life (Second Edition)*, identifies seven steps to claim authority over circumstances and be the driver of one's own career and life. Jim's third book, *The Joy of Living — Seven Steps to Give up Worry, Open Your Heart, and Love Your Life*, shows how to live a spirited adventure and joyfully play "The Game of Life." In addition, Jim has written various eBooks on living *Stress Free* and three workbooks to empower your life.

After earning his Bachelor of Arts degree in English from Franklin & Marshall College in Lancaster, PA, Jim served as a Pilot in the United States Navy. He then went on to earn his Master of Arts Degree in Applied Behavioral Science from Whitworth College in Spokane, WA. Jim now lives in Vermont where he enjoys hiking, photography, classical music and time spent with family.

For additional information regarding how your organization become stress-free, or to schedule a complimentary consultation, please contact:

Jim Koehneke, MA
jim@loveyourworktoday.com
www.loveyourworktoday.com

Please check out Jim's other books currently available at Amazon.com:

Books by Jim Koehneke

www.ingramcontent.com/pod-product-compliance
Lightning Source LLC
Chambersburg PA
CBHW060408190526
45169CB00002B/806